Russia in Transition:

Left, Right or Center?

Russia in Transition:

Left, Right or Center?

Edited by

N.G. Bugeuli

NOVA SCIENCE PUBLISHERS, INC
Commack, New York

Creative Design: Gavin Aghamore

Editorial Production: Susan Boriotti

Assistant Vice President/Art Director: Maria Ester Hawrys

Office Manager: Annette Hellinger

Graphics: Frank Grucci

Book Production: Michelle Keller, Ludmila Kwartiroff, Christine Mathosian,
Joanne Metal, Tammy Sauter and Tatiana Shohov

Circulation: Iyatunde Abdullah, Sharon Britton, and Cathy DeGregory

Library of Congress Cataloging-in-Publication Data
available upon request

ISBN 1-56072-488-9

Copyright © 1997 by Nova Science Publishers, Inc.
6080 Jericho Turnpike, Suite 207
Commack, New York 11725
Tele. 516-499-3103   Fax 516-499-3146
E-Mail: Novascience@earthlink.net

Printed in the United States of America

CONTENTS

PREFACE

This book examines the conflicting political tendencies in modern Russia to zig to the left, zag to the right or if all else fails, to drop in the center or at least to rest there for a while. This zigging and zagging is a nontrivial event at the end of the 20th century considering nuclear warheads, NATO expansion and global economic considerations.

At the moment, Russia is being handled somewhat gingerly by the West – at least during NATO's military expansion. She has been granted a short stool at the 6-7 round table, which has now been, renamed the Summit of the Eight, a label which curiously sounds like it was coined during China's Cultural Revolution.

Where does the transition in Russia lead? The answer to this question is based not only on the external influences being exerted on Russia (primarily by the United States and Germany) but also on the political values and mentality of the governing class within Russia. This book tries to probe below the surface and examine these thought patterns.

N.G. Bugeuli
July 1997

LIBERAL VALUES IN
THE MENTALITY OF RUSSIANS

Boris Kapustin[*],
Igor Klyamkin[**]

Judging by what is going on the surface of politics, a deep conflict of values is on hand in Russian society, which cannot be reduced to a conflict of economic interests. It may be assumed that this conflict exists and develops not only between "the traditional Soviet" and the liberal types of mentality, but also between various kinds of the liberal mentality proper, as well as between them and some original - not liberal, nor "traditional Soviet" world outlooks. It may also be assumed that the political culture of diverse social groups of Russian society, develops not merely by leaps and bounds, but also - in a relatively short perspective - in different directions. It may be assumed, lastly, that the ideological assimilation of the elements of the liberal world outlook is not always accompanied by a respective political behavior, this assimilation often boiling down to the learning of a fashionable lingo, effecting no substantial shifts in the mentality, and, subsequently, providing no fundamentally new visions of realities and one's attitude to them.

[*] B. Kapustin, D. Sc. (Philos.), Professor, Chief Researcher of the Fund of Social and Political Studies.
[**] I. Klyamkin, D. Sc. (Philos.), Head of the Analytical Centre of the Public Opinion Fund. The article was first published in Russian in the journal, *Polis*, No. 1, 1994.

Whether these and some other assumptions are just or unjust only time will show, as it always does. But already now we may try and test them, arriving at a more precise notion about the processes going on in society, than the one we have today. In the Autumn of 1993, an attempt was made to study especially the issue of Russians' disposition to liberal values.

First, we tried to establish, if only in the first approximation, which values – "liberal" or "socialist" were most actualized in the mentality of various groups of the population and how they correlate with each other. Secondly, a group had been singled out whose representatives identified themselves with liberalism. Having considered the particular economic and political orientations of the given group, we were able to reveal both the specific features of precisely Russian liberal (to be more exact, the one which styles itself such) mass mentality, and its profound internal contradictory nature. Thirdly, and lastly, we endeavored to clarify how Russians understand such notions as freedom, equality, tolerance, private property, the state, justice and progress – notions that are key characteristics of any world outlook, the liberal one included.

Before we start expounding the results of our investigation, we would like to characterize in greater detail the initial hypotheses by which we were guided and which we wanted to test.

Liberal values, which presuppose, in particular, the preparedness for compromises, are rather widespread in modern Russia and play a fairly significant political role. Otherwise, it would be hard to explain the main thing: why a society going through a revolution has so far succeeded in avoiding catastrophic and uncontrollable developments, localizing conflicts and armed classes both at its borders and in the small area in the centre of the capital. And this despite such powerful destructive factors as the disintegration of historical statehood, lower living standards of the majority of the population, a deep crisis of world outlooks, and the failure of the present authorities to satisfy if only one of its promises relating to the immediate interests of the rank-and-file citizens.

Many forecasts misfired, including those made by serious analysts to the effect that the collapse of former ideologically structuralized realities or, in other words, the collapse of the Soviet official Marxism in the absence of the liberal world outlook, would inevitably return Russia from the ideologically and rationally ordered world as it was after 1914 to "the classical field of history" where "more ancient, more primitive forces – nationalist and religious, fundamentalist and, in the long run, even Malthusian – will compete with each other".[1] If we add to this circumstance that the politically mobilizing slogans of anti-totalitarian reforms in Russia (and also in Eastern Europe) proved to be very near to, or identical with, the slogans of classic bourgeois revolutions in the West (people's sovereignty, the right and freedoms of men, abolition of privileges, etc.)[2] then our hypothesis about the spread in Russian society of liberal political orientations (or, at least, orientations near to them) would not at all seem too much of an exaggeration. The point is how deep these orientations are; are they not just an ideology of rejecting communism, being superficial and situational; or have they had time to strike root in the value core of the mentality?

At the present time, liberal orientations of Russian derive, as a rule, from spiritual and cultural factors, not the economic ones, including private ownership. It cannot be otherwise: for our society does not produce, nor reproduce the liberal mentality "objectively", by proxy of "existing rituals" of socio-economic and political behaviour. Today and in the foreseeable future Russia is not and will not be in structural and functional terms a liberal-democratic country: she does not have a developed market of any significance, neither a rule-of-law state in the strict sense of the term, nor does she have respective cultural institutions, beginning with the system of education.

It stands to reason, objective, above all economic, living conditions would influence the formation of liberal orientations in our country, opening up for this greater or lesser possibilities. But the position can hardly be treated as

---

[1] J. Gray, *Post-Liberalism*, New York, 1992, p. 249.

[2] This circumstance is stressed by J. Habermas. A prominent American philosopher B. Ackerman speaks about the international significance of the anti-totalitarian changes in the former Soviet bloc, he considers them exactly as "a second stage of liberal revolutions", creating for the West favourable conditions to restore "activist liberalism", which was pushed aside and overshadowed in the 19th and 20th centuries by the "liberalism of free competition" (B. Ackerman, *The Future of Liberal Revolution*, New Haven, 1992, pp. 4, 9). We shall not discuss the philosophical and historical schemes of Habermas and Ackerman, only pointing out that their propositions are important to see what, or of what type, political actions of liberalism may be, or may not be, efficient in Russia.

serious of those people who connect the prospect of the establishment of the liberal-democratic system in Russia exclusively with the development of the class of owners.

The influence of economic conditions on the formation of liberal values would rather manifest itself in the dependence on them of the accessibility for citizens of precisely non-economic, spiritual-cultural prerequisites of the liberal mentality (education, multiform and significant public contacts, the need to take responsible decisions, etc.). And if this is so, then we may assume that educational standards, types of professional activity, involvement into politics should be in closer correlation with the presence or absence of liberal orientations than, say, the enterprise where the respondent works (state-owned, joint-stock or private), his place of residence and the level of incomes.

What is more, even if we speak of private owners, this in itself does not at all mean that he or she is a vehicle of a modern liberal outlook. An owner whose mentality is alien or, at least, indifferent to the ideas of political and moral liberty and individual liberty, is no more a liberal, than a representative of any other group singled out by purely economic characteristics.

What has been said grants the assumption that today in Russia liberal orientations are inherent primarily in elite groups whose activities presuppose in the large measure the combination of higher education, the need to take responsible decisions and involvement (often forced) into politics, as well as broad and multiform "ties with people". Such an orientation may, of course, manifest itself in the given groups to the extent to which their representatives have freed themselves from communism, entertaining no hopes of its restoration, and look for different ideological, political and economic ground for the survival and the development of the country, as well as for their own self-assertion.

But a different, directly opposite conclusion is possible. Orientations of this kind are even more inherent not only in the more developed part of traditional Soviet elite which had outlives the former system of relations, but also in non-traditional groups which broke away from it, willingly or unwillingly. What we have in mind is not only entrepreneurs, but also, strange as it may seem, the unemployed.

Representatives of those groups can too much lesser degree rely on solid behaviourist and mental stereotypes, on the customary schemes of social adaptation (in this case they are joined by pupils and students). Therefore we may suppose that their perception of realities is tinged much stronger with individualism it is - liberal or non-liberal - can be established only in the course of the investigation.

As to the traditional massive groups of Russian society (industrial workers, collective-farmers and some others), we in advance disposed ourselves to adopt a specially careful and sober approach to changes occurring in their mentality. In particular, we proceeded from the fact that the seeming liberalism of many representatives of those groups, revealed in the course of numerous public opinion polls (here the share of the supporters of private property, deeper reforms, etc. was rather high) more often than not represents a specific product of the disintegration of the Soviet type of mass mentality: its disintegration is accompanied by stronger peculiarities inherent in this type of mentality, not by their disappearance. Externally it may look like negating them and turning into something fundamentally new. Thus, recognition of the very same private property may have nothing in common with the recognition of it as the object and the foundation of labour activity: in the eyes of many private property is only a supplementary source of consumer benefits and pleasures. Strictly speaking, there is nothing new in it: this trait of the Soviet mentality very much familiar to us (at least in Brezhnev's period), which changes its outer ideological coating to correspond to "the spirit of the time".

We may also assume that the varying degree with which various specific liberal values are accepted testifies to the formation of liberal mentality in post-communist Russia. In other words, some values have a greater influence on that process, possessing in that respect a considerably greater potential.

Thus, the higher degree of novelty of some values, the harder it is to identify them with the traditional Soviet values; the deeper they have struck root in the newly shaped forms of social practice, the less it is possible to accept them superficially, "verbally". In this sense, the potential of "freedom", for one, must be considerably greater than the potential of "equality" to which the ear of the Soviet man had accustomed, while that of "private property" is considerably greater than the potential of the "rule-of-law" state. Private property has already succeeded in permeating the fabrics of Russian socio-economic realities much deeper than law permeated the fabrics of political realities.

And the last hypothesis: we proceed from the fact that the presence or absence of liberal orientations in the mentality of Russians is the integrating indicators of the notions of justice and progress. Furthermore, the idea of justice is especially important because, as distinct from the idea of progress, it is always actualized in the mentality and tells on both the assessments of concrete events in life and its routine everyday course and on the nature of general judgments and contemplations about it.

The issue of justice is, in the last analysis, the issue of which type of relations between people, which kind of organization of society are acceptable to Man, urging him to fulfill his duties as a member of that society and observe the generally accepted rules, and which are not. A socium, which is fundamentally unacceptable to its population from the standpoint of the notions of justice accepted in it, just cannot exist.

If the notions of justice, which predominate in society, contain a liberal component or if they are, at least, compatible with liberalism, such a society has a chance of becoming a liberal one. And, on the contrary, it cannot become such, if, as our some liberal radicals recommend, the supporters of reforms "would give up the hypocritical and false task of regulating relations between their citizens in a socially just way".[3] Indeed, liberalism is incompatible with a communist (leveling and redistributary) version of justice. But liberalism is also incompatible with the renunciation of the idea of justice generally.

The same applies to the notion of progress. To be able to speak about preparedness or non-preparedness of Russians to accept liberal values, it would be in place to know what society they regard as being "good", a suitable one, for which one has to strive. This is especially important in transitional periods, when the notion of progress advances to the forefront.

To be able to judge more or less authentically how well liberal values adapt themselves in the mentality of the Russian population at large and in its

---

[3] *Izvestia*, August 31, 1992.

individual social groups, we must have some criterion of liberalism with which to compare the real notions of men. Let us call that criterion the ideal type of liberal mentality, using the well-known notion of Max Weber. The specific features of that type consist in that it fixes only some more essential, constitutional characteristics of the phenomenon (liberal mentality in our case), but in a most abstract, least substantial shape.

We proceed from the fact that liberal mentality of the ideal type presupposes the recognition of the self-value of individual freedom realized differently in the different spheres of life. In relations within civil society it is realized as equality in freedom, or, which is the same thing, the freedom equals (nobody may enjoy greater freedom than others may). In relations between the individual and the state, it is realized as equality before law, which guarantees the freedom of private and public activities not contradicting it. In relation to differences, to the multiformity of social life, it is realized as a tolerance to everything that does not itself negate tolerance. In economic relations it is realized as recognition of private property as a condition of Man's free development.

Even most general concepts about the evolution of liberal mentality in the modern world, on the one hand, and about the real mentality of the post-communist Russian society, on the other, are more than enough to be able to single out several types of mentality, proceeding from their distance - long or short - from the ideal type. We shall say at once that this classification does not claim to provide an exhaustive typology of the political mentality of Russians. The first type of mentality is distinguished by the non-acceptance of individual freedom as a self-value. But if the question of freedom does arise, then it is identified with equal living standard or, in other words, with the similar position of people in relation to central authorities and the distribution of benefits. This is not a liberal type of mentality, which may be called the "traditional Soviet" one. Being the product of the entire Soviet history and primarily its late (Brezhnev) period, it is characterized by developed individualism, but one of consumer-private, not productive, moral or public-political kind. This is a type of a particular man in a totalitarian-communist society where there is no private property.

People, belonging to the "traditional Soviet" type may have an orientation towards collectivism, but its semblance of the organic pre-industrial community, the community of the Russian type included, is purely exterior. There is no deep continuity here. For "collectivism" in the given case is nothing more than a specific form of the leveling organization of atomized and a political (or only ritually politicized) individuals.

Well, then, what happens in the mentality of people of the "traditional Soviet" type in conditions of a transitional society? Adapting themselves ideologically to the existing situation they may display acceptance of particular liberal values. They may lay accent on the components of their former world outlook, lessening or even removing other orientations (for instance, to increase consumer orientation and simultaneously weaken the leveling orientation which was initially conjugated with the former). They may, at least, to display specific politicization as a response to the onslaught of alternative and clearly not "Soviet" types of mentality and styles of life. As a result, the probability grows of the renaissance of the values of the early, "heroic" period of the Soviet history. True, this renaissance is inorganic, artificial, since it is rather a protective reaction of the atomized consumers whose mentality is afflicted not only by the infringement of their interests, but also by the destruction of the mode of life they have been accustomed to. As a consequence, this destruction and the resultant artificial reaction to it transform "heroic" communism into a "heroic" nationalism. Such a transformation has already surfaced in politics and it has to be examined most closely. But the "traditional Soviet" types of mentality and its modern modifications interest us only to the extent to which they oppose or imitate liberalism.

The second type of mentality presupposes the recognition of the value of individual freedom. But it is taken to mean exclusively the freedom to realize one's own interests, limited by the power of other people or circumstances, not by law. Essentially, what we have here is not individual freedom, but individual arbitrariness.

By a number of characteristics, primarily of the economic kind (private property is recognized without any reservations), this type of mentality looks like one of the subtypes of the liberal mentality of which we shall speak later on. By other criteria, fixed in the ideal type, it does not correspond to the liberal mentality, lacking the least necessary number of characteristics inherent in the liberal mentality. Let us call this type the "non-liberal individualism".

Externally, it is absolutely oppositional to the "traditional Soviet" type of mentality, being its unconditional and categoric negation. What we actually have is just one of the transformations (true, a very substantial one) of the "traditional Soviet" type, which we have mentioned in passing. What we mean is sharply strengthened consumer accents against the background of the equally sharp riddance of the leveling accents.

This type of mentality and its evolution are extremely important as regards the outlook for the market reforms that got started in Russia. It is one thing if it evolves in the direction of liberalism though nobody can say today that its vehicles would choose such a route. And it is quite a different matter if it evolves, so to say, on its own basis. Then we would be doomed to decades of criminal arbitrariness. For that reason, "non-liberal individualism" has to be treated with utmost seriousness.

And, lastly, the liberal type of mentality: it can be subdivided into two subtypes – "economically liberal" and "socially liberal". Furthermore, we shall consider them as two independent types for the sake of convenience, but we ask the reader not to forget their "paradigm" kinship.

The basic difference between those types may be illustrated, using aphoristic formulation of the classics of liberal thought. According to L. von Muses (he represents, if we use our classification, the "economic" liberalism), "the programme of liberalism… if it is condensed in one word, would read: property".[4]

Externally, it really resembles what we called "non-liberal individualism". But it does so only externally. The thing is that with Muses all other liberal values (political and civil freedom, tolerance, etc.) do not stand on a par with private property, but do necessarily flow from it. There are no, nor can there be contradictions between the principle of private property (if it is realized consistently) and all the other rights and freedoms of Man: by definition, private ownership is justified and is expedient, proceeding from the general, not

---

[4] L. von Muses, *Liberalism in Classical Tradition*, New York, 1984, p. 19.

the private interests of a liberal society. As to the "non-liberal individualism", it not only allows for such contradictions, but readily reconciliates with them. This is its practically basic manifestation as being not liberal.

Now about "social liberalism". It gives priority to freedom, not private property, allowing for the possibility of its conflict with other values. Such a conflict must unfailing be resolved in favour of freedom. It is worthwhile noticing that this version of liberalism presupposes the use of various means to realize and develop freedom under the circumstances of place and time. Meanwhile, "economic" liberalism, which is headed in terms of values by private property, takes advantage of it as a universal practical means of realizing any other values.

And, lastly, fairly subtle differences are manifested between the two versions of liberalism concerning the very essence of particular values and the crisis crossing of their meanings. Let us take, for instance, freedom and equality. In the eyes of an "economic liberal", equality is a value inasmuch as it comes forward as a condition of realizing freedom, which, in the given case, means primarily the freedom of property. Therefore, the idea of equality before law (both as a juridical norm and as the law of the functioning of the market economy) is near and dear to the "economic liberal". Any other additions to this - minimally liberal - interpretation of equality are, however, rejected.

A "social liberal" would, of course, hardly argue against such an interpretation of equality corresponding to the spirit of liberal mentality. He would not even be tempted into modifying it in the spirit of leveling. But he sees the problem where the "economic liberal" sees none. The crux of the problem lies in that adhering to the position of "minimal" equality, one just cannot secure that very "minimal" equality

A typical example: equality before the market presupposes the equality of starting conditions of each new generation. But the market laws do not stipulate it at all, what is more they, as we know, are conducive to greater not lesser inequality from generation to generation. In order to remove or, at least, mitigate the given contradiction, "social liberalism" supplements the formula flowing from the "minimal" equality version with demands for equal starting opportunities capable of finding and opening up talents. In the practical language it implies the implementation of respective programmes in the sphere of education, public health and social security.

On the other hand, a "social liberal" evaluates equality not merely as a condition of realizing freedom. For him it carries its own independent message, since a greater zone of equality is simultaneously a greater volume and a richer content of freedom. He deems it necessary to expand and strengthen the spheres and basics of equality, not their narrowing and reduction to the margins accessible to the less advanced layers of the given society socially and culturally. For his part, the "economic" liberal also does not wish to orient himself on these layers, he is mainly concerned with defending himself and his world outlook from their peculiar treatment of equality. He does not see any other problem here at all. Therefore, it would not be exaggerating things if we say that the essential pathos of that position in developed countries is projected either into the present (as opposition to the leveling) or into the past (overcoming mediaeval Estate privileges), not into the future.

As to Russia which emerges from the epoch of communist leveling practices and communist privileges, here things are quite different: in Russia the issue of the near future of not only this or that version of liberalism, but of liberalism generally is still open. At the same time, as the reader will see, our data make it possible to voice on those scores certain suppositions.

From what has been said it follows, that the "social-liberal" mentality implies that the development of equality does not undermine the historically won positions of freedom.

Now, let us see what happens on the surface of mentality, not raising the question of what it is capable or incapable potentially.

The real essence of liberal values in the mentality of our citizens, their real dynamics manifests itself more distinctly if we compare the perception of these values with the perception of traditional Soviet values, opposing them, as well as with some other values forming the background where such an opposition stands in bolder relief. In particular, we shall deal at length with the attitude to a value expressed by the word "work" (its rating, as we shall see, is very important to understand the deep-rootedness of modern mass mentality in the communist past) and the word "professionalism" (this word fixes - at the first approximation - the extent of deideologization and, subsequently rationalization of the mentality, defining the role and place of the very same work). Of equal interest, we believe, is the reaction to the word "spirituality" (some analysts say that in modern discussions "opposition of freedom to spirituality" is to be observed), the word "dignity" (without the idea of personal dignity, the liberal idea of the independence of the individual from the state loses moral, and consequently, liberal sense), and, lastly, the words "family" and "decent living". Their comparison with liberal values would help to understand whether the private life of post-Soviet man is filled with liberal values or whether it rejects them. This is the way these values correlate in various social groups.

Here the difference is shown (in per cent) between the shares of supporters of particular values among the population as a whole and in individual social groups.

It is not hard to notice that at this level of the analysis our initial hypotheses are corroborated only in part. Of all the values we are interested in only freedom and justice are actualized to a varying degree: the rest - progress, equality, property, tolerance are still in the periphery of the mentality. This does not mean that people do not accept them cannot accept them generally. It only means that today they do not appreciate them as they should. The varying role of various values in forming the liberal mentality is also one of our hypotheses and the data received do not repudiate it.

To a certain extent was corroborated our proposition that the elite groups, and not only new, but also the old ones, are more open to accept liberal values. True, the rating of freedom among the representatives of massive groups. But the attitude to property, say, of directors (and they are the only group in this respect) is somewhat more favorable and more grounded than among the massive layers of the population.

And yet the data received gives no ground for optimism. What troubles one is somewhat constrained attitude of most elite groups to justice as compared with the bulk of the population. Anxiety is caused by what should in all probability inspire one: a high (especially high in all elite groups) rating of law - a higher demand for law on the background of rather weakly actualized other liberal values, testifies to anything, but not to an accelerated advance in the direction of liberal lawful state.

And if this is so, the revealed hierarchy of actual preferences is interesting not as such, but as a material making it possible to put forth some suppositions about the concrete essence of those preferences.

Today in the mentality of Russians are actualized primarily those values which in one way or another are connected with the activity of the state. First among them is law (if not in all groups then in many of them). Its promotion to a leading role demonstrates most graphically the transitional period we are going through, when society is in some indefinite-intermediary state: the traditional Soviet way of life has been practically destroyed, while its liberal alternative can be hardly seen.

The demand for law is the demand for the stable rules of the game, for sure guarantees that changes would not throw the mass of the people from the customary living niches, the demand for being protected, for safety in the broadest sense of the word (hence the high rating of the word "security"). And it is not all surprising that the old and the new elite groups are most of all concerned with the problem law: economic executives and managers mean by this the doctoring of the rules of the game governing their activities, while the military mean by this the protection of their status and the entire way of life from being destroyed which they regard as being "unlawful". We stress that they regard it not as unjust (the value of justice with them is lower than the average for the whole population) but as exactly unlawful, which demonstrates their preparedness to talk from the positions of strength, not weakness that usually appeals to justice.

But if we can see in all this the symptoms of liberalism, then they are very weak. At any rate, mentality of this kind may develop in a perfectly different direction, to which Russia is more used, when "law" secures the rule of the state over society. The rather high degree of the actualization of the value of freedom imbues one with the hope that there would be no comeback to the past. On the other hand, a weak actualization of the value of private property at best testifies that we still have time for these two values drawing closer together. In the worse case, the value of freedom would be either ousted from the mentality, or it would be again governmentalized (for even during the Soviet regime the official status of that value was extremely high). And then, the ream of a liberal and rule-of-law state would have to be postponed to better times.

For such a state must be rooted in private law, and, in the first place, in the right of property. So far the values of law, freedom and property begin to approximate each other only in the mentality of businessmen and farmers. Individual groups of directors develop in the same direction, but here we should not entertain any illusions: the victory of liberalism in one or several social groups, taken singly in conditions of non-liberalism of the rest of society is a Utopia.

The picture would not be so gloomy if we offer our respondents to choose not some values most cherished by them, but would try to reveal what they agree with in principle, what are they prepared to reconcile themselves with and what they cannot just concede to. So, in what combination does the idea of law and the idea of the private law stand in their mentality if they choose both?

We were able to learn this offering the respondents to pinpoint in the list of actions (which the population expects from the policy-makers) those actions with which they agree. Among other actions we proposed to them to evaluate two actions, formulated as the demands for policy-makers: "Secure a strict observance of laws" and "Guarantee the possession of private property". Here are the results.

As we can see, in the average of the population and in most social groups (barring pensioners and collective-farmers) over 40 per cent are prepared to accept the idea of private property and the idea of its juridical protection. Furthermore, in the elite groups (directors, managers, not to speak of the representatives of the private sector), these ideas, whose liberal nature is indisputable, are more widespread than in massive groups. But would this preparedness turns into a value depends primarily on how the real expansion of the layer of owners would proceed and on their influence on the social position and living standards of those who are not owners and are not going to become ones. Meanwhile, we can only speak of the embryonic state of liberalism, now knowing for sure whether it would develop, and if it would, what direction it

Table 1

Liberal and Some Other Values in the Mentality of Russians

	Law	Security	Family	Work	Justice	Decent Living	Freedom	Spirituality	Progress	Democracy	Professionalism	Equality	The Power	Dignity	Property	Tolerance
Population as a Whole	52	48	46	42	37	37	32	26	20	18	15	15	14	13	12	6
Workers	3	1	2	−3	−1	8	4	−6	0	−1	−3	2	2	2	−1	−1
Collective-farmers	−2	−4	6	5	4	6	3	−14	−1	−1	−5	2	0	5	1	4
Employees Paid from the Budget	4	1	4	−2	−2	−6	−3	6	1	−4	4	−2	−1	−2	1	−1
Directors	15	−8	−10	3	−8	−6	4	8	3	14	17	−4	1	3	8	4
Chairmen	13	−7	1	8	0	−2	5	−8	−6	6	0	0	5	−1	2	1
Managers	19	−13	−3	−2	0	−8	−4	15	6	13	6	−4	0	4	3	1
Officers	17	11	−6	−12	−7	−10	5	2	3	1	21	−10	14	5	−3	−1
Businessmen	13	−4	−4	−15	−17	−5	18	7	3	19	10	−9	1	1	14	3
Farmers	3	−5	−2	−7	−6	0	10	0	−4	22	6	−2	1	2	26	−3
Unemployed	7	11	4	−1	2	4	−1	−2	1	3	−2	−5	−4	1	2	4
Pensioners	1	−1	−5	12	6	−4	−12	−1	5	−3	−4	1	2	0	−5	2
Students	−6	−5	−4	−9	−2	−4	17	3	0	−4	6	−1	0	2	7	1

would take.

We should not lose sight of the fact that practically in all massive groups over half the respondents (and over two-thirds among pensioners and collective-farmers) have not voiced their agreement to the guarantees for owners. Another thing is also important, calling for attention: general demand to strengthen law is 50, 100 (and even 150 per cent) higher than the demand to protect property. An inverse dependence we can only observe in the groups of businessmen and farmers, as well as among pupils and students whose ideology stems not from their economic and social position and interests thereof, but primarily from their age.

Therefore, we have all grounds to assume that in the mentality of the post-Soviet man, all the recent ideological shifts notwithstanding, predominant are still the notions of law, associated with the customary functions of the former state as a guarantee of social order in conditions where productive private interests are not yet developed and differentiated. A private person (or a community of people) who had been molded in the Soviet years see in another private person (or a community of people) a rival exclusively in consumption, not in production. In a society where all sources and functions of development had been concentrated in the hands of the state, in a society, which endeavoured to develop economically, and technologically without the institution of private property, such state of affairs was inevitable.

Hence such a specific feature of the post-Soviet man as orientation towards private life, the welfare of the family and a decent living (see Table 1), while orientation towards property is expressed weakly, remaining in the periphery of mentality. In the mentality of the post-Soviet man the place of the latter orientation is still held by the state. A comparatively high rating of justice in massive groups is also nothing else than the continued manifestation of that orientation; weak roots of the value of the right to property, its non-actualization is compensated for by high moral expectations and demands made not so much on themselves or some other people, but on the very same state. From what has been said it follows that if some prerequisites of liberalism do not take shape in Russia which experiences the collapse of the Soviet mentality, then these are yet prerequisites of "Social" liberalism, and by no means of an "economic" liberalism.

Less of all we would like to be understood in the sense that "Social liberalism" would make it possible to resolve quickly the problems our "economic liberals" have failed to cope with. Furthermore, the problems cropping up on this road are colossal intricate and new: for "social liberalism" envisages the re-distribution of the wealth, but for this one must have what to re-distribute. "Social liberalism" of today's poor country with weakened and deranged state into the bargain, has no precedent in history. At present we wish to fix the real choice the country has to make either "social liberalism" or some kind of "national-socialism".

It is from the standpoint of this real alternative, of this real and not invented choice we would have to make, that we are going to consider the values of the post-Soviet society: under the circumstances they would be playing the role which is far from being the last. And what should interest us in the first place is justice, which plays a leading role both in the ensemble of "social-liberal" values and in the ideological concepts fundamentally opposed to liberalism.

We have already dealt with data testifying to a fairly high rating of justice among the massive layers of the population and to a lower interest in it not only among businessmen and farmers, but also among such groups as the directors and the military. Apparently the representatives of the private sector associate the word "justice" with that glorious past when everything that was spearheaded against property and proprietors, and with that present time when excessive, in their view, taxes are levied on them. High taxes are also most likely to tell on the attitude of directors to justice. One of two conclusions is possible here: either the representatives of those groups are wary of the past, "communist" version of justice (or then their evolution towards "social-liberalism" is quite possible) or by justice is meant something else.

As to the military, the lower rating of the word justice with them has a direct bearing, in our view, on the specific response, typical only of the officers, to their lost status; they regard this not as injustice, but as an "unlawful" infringement of not merely their own, but of state interests.

Even more instructive in this respect is the attitude of the military to such a value as equality. It is only among businessmen, whom the word "equality" cannot but remind of the former system where the business activity just could not take place because of its incompatibility with the official deal of "social equality", that the attitude to that value is just as indifferent as among the military.

Why, then, does the idea of equality, which was a most attractive idea in past liberal revolutions, look absolutely differently in the present revolutionary epoch? Evidently, the thing is that at that time idea of equality was spearheaded against Estate privileges (equality before the law). As to the Communist regime, there nobody had any formal juridical privileges and the "fight against privileges" and the promotion of the idea of equality stood in no need. What is more, anti-communists had to fight on two fronts: against the privileges of Nomenclature high-ranking government and Party officials and against the leveling trends. But for this they needed not the idea of equality, but the idea of inequality, which they had, perhaps for the first time in history, to romanticize among the popular masses, not the elite.

The military, for their part, are not enthusiastic about the word "equality" for a different reason: after the collapse of communism they feel very much like the representatives of the high strata of feudal society felt after they had been deprived of their special status. This analogy is, of course, very conventional, but it helps one grasp what is going on among the officers. In the Soviet militarized system the military, unlike other groups, had all grounds to identify themselves with the state. And today they expect from the state not so much justice and equality as the return of their "lawful" guarantees of their specific status, which stems from their understanding of their special role as a government Estate. They even do not consider the state as a tool of their individual and group interests wishing for their identification, their symbiosis with the state – at least ideologically.

It is possibly thanks to this that the officers are the only group, which perceives the image of the state as something concrete. In all other groups this image is eroded and devoid of definiteness. The specificity of the present moment consists in that by inertia people expect from the state something customary and familiar as was the case in the past decades, having no idea what the state can and must be in the changed conditions.

On the one hand, the new statehood is not perceived as a direct continuation, and still less the restoration, of the former state: the rating of the word "power" is exceedingly low in all groups (except, of course, the military). But the image of the fundamentally new, democratic statehood had not yet taken shape in the mass mentality, evidence of which is the low rating of the word "democracy" (see Table 1). And, at the same time, it is exactly democracy, not the "power" that causes the heightened interest not only in new elite groups, which is perfectly natural, but also in old elite groups (again excepting the military).

And so, what we see in most old elite groups is a very high demand for law and a heightened interest in democracy. This corroborates our hypothesis that in the elite groups the cultural and political prerequisites for liberalism are formed faster than in the massive groups. This is evidence that in the mentality of the elite the image of future statehood has not yet been formed clearly and specifically, but the desire to have it is much stronger than in the massive layers of the population; at the same time elite fears that it would be an ideologized statehood. This is especially noticeable among the directors. It is worthwhile to point out that it was the only group where the word "democracy" has a higher rating than the word "might". This information merits attention, we should not consider the comparisons of these two ratings to be too indiscreet. And the thing is that such a comparison reveals a striking difference between the directors and the military (among the latter the share of those supporting "might" is 350 per cent higher than that of the supporters of "democracy"). The thing is that the directors differ greatly in this respect from the population as a whole, where the rating of "might" is two times higher than the rating of "democracy".

What we see here is an accelerated deidelogization of the Directors' Corps, or, at any rate, an accelerated getting rid of the ideologization of the "traditional Soviet" type. The massive layers are much tardier in doing so. But in their mentality the eroded former notions still persist in the shape of most general ideologems. As to the "specificity", it is being ousted very rapidly.

It is instructive that the rating of "might" among the Russian population is three times higher than the rating of "power". Apparently, the notion of the grandeur of the country has been preserved in the massive mentality, as has also been the desire to restore it, but this time without the former communist-military form, but as something new, which has not yet been found. And it can be sought either in liberalism (economic might in place of the former purely military might) or in nationalism, which continues traditionally to lay emphasis on the military might. But here, too, the prospect of liberalism again depends on its ability to become in our condition "social-liberalism".

For that reason, the notion of security may assume with us a perfectly special significance. Unlike all other notions, it fixes the continuity of the "Soviet traditional" type of mentality and - simultaneously - it harbours an alternative to it. It bespeaks the nostalgic reminiscences of the totalitarian establishment and the traces of the "defensive mentality", but at the same time, it is marked by the idea of the protection of the individual who has had a taste of freedom, by the protection in the broadest sense of the word, including his protection against the arbitrariness of the state. It contains a rare combination of the synthetic content of world outlook and the situational political, everyday life meaning. But we should not forget: if security and freedom fail to unite in a liberal synthesis, if they fail to supplement each other, then the idea of security may well combine with the need for a new ideologized non-freedom the "national-socialist" kind.

The danger of this course of developments remains considerable. And one of the reasons for this is that the potential demand for freedom is not accompanied by the preparedness of the mass mentality to master the space of freedom. The split between the individual and the state, the molding of a special variety of person who is ideologically independent of the ideologized state - a process that began in Brezhnev's epoch and had been completed by the Perestroika times, does not lead so far (or leads to an insignificant extent) to the emergence of a personality who is really independent of the state, it does not lead to the division between private and state vital activities. And this is only natural: so long as the idea of property and its inviolability has not struck root in society, a private person remains an atomized individual, devoid of any stable organic ties with other individuals like he himself. Hence two unavoidable consequences: the preservation (not always clearly expressed) of the demand for a universal "go-between", whose function in the former system was discharged by the state ("the State - the Party") and the undeveloped state of private - especially productive - interests.

If the idea of property has practically not been actualized in mentality, nor has been actualized such a liberal value as tolerance. The alarmingly low and almost the same rating of that value in all the groups bespeaks not only the considerable potential of intolerance, but also the fact the issue of tolerance is simply absent due to the undeveloped and non-differentiated state of private interests and to the lack of inter-group contradictions or contradictions between individuals, the word does not touch a responsive cord in the mentality of people.

This does not mean that Russian society is anti-liberal. It means, that it responded in the person of its considerable part of representatives to the idea of freedom, remains all the same a pre-liberal society which still has to make its choice between a liberal and non-liberal route of development.

It is instructive that such liberal values as property and tolerance have not practically been actualized in the mass mentality. The notion of dignity - that major sign of the independent individual and its high status as a private person - has also been actualized very weakly. It is even more characteristic that representatives of private-property sector do not differ at all in this respect from the other groups. This is an important symptom that they are not prepared for the role of a social leader in the broadest sense of the word, which, in turn, presupposes a moral leadership; here one can readily see the manifestation of their dependence and non-freedom. It looks like the majority of Russian owners still stay in the value field of "non-liberal individualism", which is either not sensitive to the moral side of the matter, or becomes a conscious successor of the amorality of the former system which it opposes.

We have to reckon with all this, if we want to see the place and role in the Russian mentality of one of the fundamental liberal values – a basic value in "social liberalism" – the value of freedom. The very fact that the greatest significance is attached to it precisely in the business and farmers' groups, gives food to the thought that freedom in modern Russia is primarily a negative value, a "freedom from" (totalitarianism), not yet a "freedom for". A high rating of freedom among pupils and students does not contradict this, though in the given case the general anti-totalitarian motivations are supplemented, evidently, by the age-grounded hostility to all regulation.

True, it may seem that against the background of the low status of property, tolerance and dignity, some positive essence of freedom can still be seen. It can be seen not so much in economic, social, political or moral orientations as in some spiritual-cultural strivings in a most general, ideal and abstract sense. For instance, it is indisputable that in the Russian mentality freedom merges with spirituality - and this despite the fact that in some intellectual quarters these values are considered as antagonists: the former as predominantly "Western", and the latter as "the originally native". In the eyes of those for whom spirituality is a value it is not a symbol of allegiance to exclusively national religious orthodox tradition (as distinct from freedom, as a symbol of denouncing it sharply). Both values are likely to be viewed as values opposing the "traditional Soviet" values, supplementing each other in this sense. From this standpoint, spirituality becomes a kind of a synthesis of allegiance to native pre-revolutionary culture and modern Western culture. But if our supposition is correct, that means that in present condition spirituality, just as freedom, is primarily a negative value, rather rejecting the old content than asserting the new one.

The positive content of freedom (and spirituality, too) can only be attained not as a result of increasing the force of rejecting non-freedom, but as a result of accelerating in the space of freedom of that heritage that was bequeathed to us from the Soviet epoch. In this sense, it is much more important to single out not those values that supplement freedom, but the values that contradict it. Essentially, the problem is to what extent that contradiction is organic, to what extent is different sides are capable of coexisting peacefully and developing side by side, not transpassing the boundary beyond which the struggle of destruction starts, i.e., till the complete victory of one of these sides.

Today freedom opposes justice. In its nature this value is not at all alien to liberalism, being used as an ideological shield to protect primarily the vehicles of "traditional Soviet" values (their highest rating is among pensioners and collective-farmers) and, as we have already said, it is accepted with greater restraint in groups opposing them (the lowest rating of justice is among businessmen).

Another demarcation line of fundamental significance runs between "freedom-work". If the high rating of freedom is the product of the degovernmentalization of the individual that started in Brezhnev's epoch by the actual deideologization of the family (and the private life generally), which later on was supplemented by degovernmentalization of political sphere, the freeing of man as a voter and broadly, as a citizen, a still higher rating of the work is a consequence of processes (more exactly - their absence) of a perfectly different kind. The thing is that degovernmentalization of the economic and social spheres (as distinct from the ideological and political ones) have not so far taken place. What is more, people, as a rule, do not accept the way the degovernmentalization proceeds. This is manifested, on the one hand, in a weak actualization of the value of property, and a strong actualization of the value of work.

This does not mean, that freedom and work are perceived in the mentality as exclusively antagonistic values: often they are reconciled (the ideal of "free" work). Among those who indicated freedom among main values, 33 per cent simultaneously indicated as such work (for the population as a whole, the figure was 42 per cent), while among those who opted for work, 24 per cent simultaneously opted for freedom (among the population as a whole the figure was 32 per cent). These overlappings are of certain interest, since simultaneous recognition of the value work/freedom in our conditions may be evidence of the purely "Soviet" understanding of the freedom of work, i.e., freedom from discipline, responsibility, rigid hierarchic subordination, professionalism. But this reconciliation is far from being implemented on a somewhat large-scale, becoming a solid stable and durable socio-economic reality. An indirect corroboration of the opposition of work to freedom (exactly as different values) is the fact that the former has the greatest appeal in the eyes of pensioners, i.e., those who no longer work, while the second one is less attractive... also to pensioners. If we add to this fact that the lowest rating of work is observed among businessmen who have the highest rating in that of freedom, we may conclude that along the "work-freedom" line we observe the opposition of "traditional Soviet" and other values, the liberal values included. And this is no exaggeration.

A high status of work is an unconscious orientation of the broad layers of Russian society towards the governmentalized socio-economic sphere or, if you like, towards a governmentalized civil society. Work is a sort of a middle man between the family and the private life, which is separated ideologically and politically from the state, and the very same state to separate from which economically and socially was much harder. Many still perceive work as a guaranteed source of survival and sufficiency, as a certain substance devoid of any qualitative characteristics, which it does not suppose to have.

In this way, work is a point where the individual and the state still come into touch, while its high rating manifests their inseparability in the mentality of many people. What we have here is not an instinctive defense from future unemployment (the unemployed, by the by, do not differ in this respect from the working employees), but the recognition of the state as a job-giver – not a monopolist one as before, but still the basic one.

This value of work that has been preserved hitherto does not have anything in common with some official Soviet values, say, "collectivism" which some try to reanimate or romanticize. The rating of the latter value is practically nil in all the social groups. This is the question of the state-organized work, which is indispensable in the "heroic" epoch, while in the non-heroic epoch it fully meets the specific consumer individual needs of the Soviet and post-Soviet man.

If our considerations and suppositions are just, then we may state with a great degree of confidence: the main problem which social-liberalism" would have to face in Russia would be exactly the problem of work and its combination with freedom. The colossal difficulty of such a combination is that these two values cannot, strictly speaking, be combined: for freedom means nothing else than freedom from work in the sense in which it continues to exist. How can it be done (if it can be done at all) gradually, evolutionarily and safely for one and all – this is today the crux of the problem. Freedom-property-work-security – such is today the only possible (though very vulnerable by all classical canons) formula of liberalism in our conditions in the foreseeable period.

Having elucidated the extent of actualization of basic liberal and some non-liberal values in the mentality of Russians we may pass to the next and more specific level of analysis.

No matter how important the role of the elite may be, the future of liberalism will be decided in the massive layers, in the thick of people's life. And to be able to understand better how it will be decided, it is desirable not only to know the attitudes of workers, collective-farmers or, say, pensioners to some or other liberal or non-liberal values, but also to know something else, namely, what liberal ideology is and what it turns into after it gets into the massive mentality of present-day Russians? What are its distinctive features and contradictions? For if that ideology is destined to disseminate in width, the forms it will be taking, would hardly differ from those in which it exists today in the mentality of a comparatively small, but not elite layer. Therefore, the question of what massive liberal mentality is today in Russia is at once the question of what it may, or may not, become tomorrow.

This is the reason why we decided to deal if only briefly with the peculiarities of mentality of the people who themselves consider their views to be liberal ones or near to such. We can do this basing ourselves on the data retrieved from the answers of the respondents to the question of their confidence in the representatives of ideological and political movements. We shall remind the reader that the number of the confirmed supporters of liberalism amounted to a mere 4 per cent of all the respondents. Furthermore for the sake of convenience we shall call them "liberals", and all the rest – "non liberals".

Among the "liberals" we encounter more often than not executives of varying ranks, even more often experts with higher education (21 per cent as against 13 per cent among the "non-liberals"), school pupils and college students (13 and 5 per cent respectively) and employees working at private enterprises (10 and 5 per cent). As to the workers, collective-farmers and especially pensioners, their numbers opting for these values are much lesser.

They also differ from the rest by their income levels – true not from people with low wages, but from relatively highly paid employees, who account for a considerable share among the "liberals". This, however, does not tell very strongly on their appraisal of their own material position: though in the group of "liberals" people are met more often who class themselves among the rich or highly paid, they, however, are not very numerous (only every twentieth). Most of them consider themselves medium- or low-paid, almost not differing in this respect from the rest, and roughly every tenth (the difference from the rest is again minimal) considers himself to be poor. A certain inconsistency between the income levels and the appraisals of one's own material positions among the "liberals" are, possibly, due to their more developed needs than in other groups.

If we are to speak about the economic and political positions of the representatives of the group in question, their main distinctive feature is that their attitudes to everything connected with the reforms and reformers are better than those of the rest are. This equally applies to privatization of state-owned property, the economic independence of the individual from the state. They also constitute the majority of those who orient themselves on the West and the statesmen of the Western type. But taken by itself, it is at best evidence that the "liberals" departed farther than the rest from the aims and values of the individual of a "traditional Soviet" type, saying nothing about what is opposed to those aims and values. To disclose it, let us see how the values we spoke about earlier correlate in the mentality of "liberals" and "non-liberals".

As can be seen from the table the ousting of some old values and the filling of the vacant space with new values proceeds much faster in the mentality of "liberals" than "non-liberals". Not only "freedom" but also such words-values as "property" and "professionalism" evoke greater interest among "liberals" than among "non-liberals", and a higher rating of "spirituality" reaffirms what has been said above: spirituality is perceived not as an alternative to freedom; on the contrary, together with freedom it comes forward as an alternative to "traditional Soviet" values.

This keen interest in spirituality is manifested indirectly and, at first glance, unexpectedly in the attitude to decent living: its value in the eyes of "liberals" is noticeably lower than in the eyes of the rest respondents. This does not mean that the interests of private life are alien to them: the rating of the word "family" is even higher among them than among "non-liberals". Evidently, the thing is that individual freedom, private life protected from the interference of the state, spirituality – are for them primarily ideological symbols, with the help of which they not only reject the values of the former system, but also fix for themselves (and, perhaps, for others, too) the principled selfishness of such a rejection, its high idealism, which is alien to the considerations of personal welfare. In other words, the idea of private life is separated from the idea of private gain.

We should necessarily bear in mind this heightened ideologization of the mentality of "liberals", if we want to visualize the prospects of liberalism in this country. So far it is extremely abstract and is weakly rooted in the very same private life and private property, which are made the corner stone of their ideology. But we have now all reasons to state that our hypothesis about the extra-economic, predominantly cultural-spiritual nature of the liberal mentality in the post-communist Russia has not been groundless.

At the same time, on the ideological level the "liberals" have mastered the idea of the proprietary rights much better than others: their higher rating of "law" is not merely a reaction to the collapse of order and to lawlessness, but an ideological directive to rapidly transform the old order into a new one and its consolidation by liberal laws. For that reason in their mentality, unlike that of "non-liberals" there is practically no gap between the demand "to observe strictly the laws" (70 per cent) and "to guarantee the possession of private property" (61 per cent).

In this respect "liberals" are in a closer touch with the representatives of a new economic system, but unlike the latter, the idea of the right to property has not struck root in their private interests and their direct activities. Here they resemble not so much the businessmen and farmers as the school pupils and students with their juvenile cult of novelty.

"Liberals" resemble businessmen by a different characteristic – their attitude to the notion of "property". In both cases its rating is higher than the respective rating for the population as a whole, but it is not as high as one could have expected. As to the businessmen, this derives in all probability from the fact that they already possess property and their aim is to protect and multiply it. As to the "liberals", they, as a rule, have no property. And if its value is actualized in the mentality of every fourth, that means that the rest are not going to become proprietors. Therefore, when the majority of them, not unlike the businessmen and farmers, oppose the infringement of the right of owners and favor reliable guarantees of the inviolability of property, they thereby express ideological solidarity with the owners, hoping, evidently, that the social, economic and legislative assertion of the latter fully meets the interests of "liberals".

In short, they do not sacrifice their interests, but ideologically advance them to those who, in their view, would satisfy these interests better than the state. At the same time, their enthusiasm is backed up by the fact that in their own eyes they see themselves concerned not with their own property or somebody else's welfare, but with the well-being of one and all, defending it from the few who encroach on it. But there should be no illusions: great concern for the protection and multiplication of somebody else's property and indifference to one's own earnings may be only temporary; such an idealization of changes may go on so long as the threat of the restoration of the old economic system and way of life persists.

"Liberal's" attitude to justice is also very instructive. It again is exactly tantamount to that of the businessmen. That value is actualized very weakly in both groups. If we recall what had been said above to the effect that there can be liberalism without or outside justice, only one conclusion is possible: people, who sympathize most of all with that political and ideological movement, should interest us not merely as some liberal vanguard which it would be good to augment, but primarily as a group where not only present-day contradictions are manifested strikingly, but collisions of values of tomorrow and the day after tomorrow can be anticipated in advance.

We have already said why businessmen distance themselves from the idea of justice: evidently in their eyes it symbolizes a way of life where a "just" redistribution was incompatible with the idea of freedom, nor with the idea of private property. In this respect, too, "liberals" only express their ideological solidarity with the representatives of the private sector, believing, of course, that they voice the opinion of all or of the overwhelming majority. But, as distinct from the businessmen, their weak actualization of the idea of justice

Table 2

Values of "State" and "Private"
Law in the Mentality of Russians
(in per cent)

Actions expected from Policy-Makers	Population as a Whole	Directors	Managers	Officers	Chairmen	Unemployed	Workers	Pensioners	Collective-farmers	Employees paid from the Budget	Businessmen	Farmers	Students
Secure a strict observance of laws	66	87	86	82	75	72	72	69	67	67	67	64	54
Guarantee the possession of private property	43	57	54	48	41	48	46	29	31	50	76	69	59

Table 3

Liberal and Some Other Values in the Mentality
of "Liberals" and "Non-Liberals"
(in per cent)

	Law	Family	Freedom	Security	Spirituality	Work	Progress	Professionalism	Decent Living	Property	Justice	Democracy	Power	Equality	Dignity	Tolerance
"Liberals"	62	50	48	42	42	41	30	29	27	24	20	19	10	9	7	6
"Non-Liberals"	52	46	31	48	26	43	20	14	38	12	37	17	14	15	13	6

maybe just as temporary, as the weak actualization of the value of "decent living".

In the eyes of "liberals" justice is a value on which the old system had rested. But we shall demonstrate later on that they see it not in a traditionally Soviet sense, but fundamentally differently: not as a re-distribution in condition of state-owned property, but such a re-distribution whose vector is directed from owners to non-owners. And they treat such way of re-distribution more than favourably.

And this, in turn, signifies that their taking no interest in justice as such is not only rejection of the past, but also the vague demand for the future. But as the future turns into present, i.e., as the owners would be taking hold of the leverage of real economic and political power, the attitude of the "liberals" to justice generally will also be changing. Then it would become crystal clear that they at best seem to be supporters of "economic liberalism", while actually they may accept only "social" liberalism.

Incidentally, something else would also become clear, namely that the ideological enthusiasm about liberalism can, under certain circumstances, become a dominant of the mentality which is a far cry from liberalism.

Pay attention to the practically zero rating of tolerance in that milieu: it is exactly the same as among the "non-liberals". It is possible that tolerance is not being actualized so long as accounts have not been settled with the past, the new realities have not grown stronger, asserting themselves. That is the reason why that value is not considered as an important one. But if it is not considered such at the given moment, where is the guarantee that it would be appreciated at a later date, when contradictions of interests become sharper and more clear-cut?

But this is not the whole point. It is surprising, but yet it is a fact: our "liberals" do not care a fig for such a value as dignity: in this respect they are lesser liberals than the rest. But how, then, can the cult of freedom and spirituality be commensurated with the indifference for personal dignity?

Evidently, we observe here the peculiarities (which were pointed out already by the authors of *Vekhi*) of an ideologized mentality, which concentrates on exterior circumstances of existence (economic, political, and ideological) and the need to change them, being oblivious of personality, its inner state and quality. At the times of *Vekhi* this pathos of changing the world was aimed largely against liberalism. Now it is aimed against those who do not accept liberalism. But the essence is one and the same: the personality is dissolved ideologically in circumstance. It is interesting that here even such a personal quality as spirituality can be objectified, turning in one of useful "circumstances" which would have to replace "harmful" circumstances.

But people who sympathize with liberals (or who consider themselves as liberals) evoke interest not only by all this. They exemplify the contradictions of nascent liberal mentality in society where heightened ideologization (in the sense of rejecting the Soviet system) commensurates with heightened rationalism, evidence of which can be seen in a fairly high rating of the word "professionalism". The question, however, is what lies behind it: is it actual preparedness and ability to establish rational relations and conduct rational activities even if the necessary conditions for it are lacking, or do we again have a mere ideology of rationalism?

The materials at our disposal do not enable us to give an unambiguous answer to that question. But we have sufficient data to be doubtful about the radicalism and practical orientation of this rationalism. The thing is that the newly declared values have not struck strong roots, which results in the most fundamental values of the past, which are rejected, still persisting. Secondly, we also witness disappointment in values, whose contents have partly manifested them in life.

What merits attention is the high rating among "liberals" of the word "work" (it is almost the same as among the "non-liberals") and the low rating of the word "democracy" (a similar case with the "non-liberals"). Attitudes to work show that the representatives of the group concerned have not gone too far from the past, as one could expect using some ideological notions ("work" generally is evaluated higher than, say, property or "professionalism"). As to a not very high rating of democracy, this above all bespeaks the fact that the "liberals" who now exist in a vacuum between the past and the future, are apt to become disillusioned with the ideas which, touching the life, do not produce results expected of them.

In this way, as regards democracy substantial divergences are to be observed between "liberals", who pin their hopes on the private sector, and the representatives of this very sector. As the economy based on private property gains momentum, cannot such divergences emerge on some other issues?

It is not rule out that even now "liberals" experience internal discomfort. The speed of parting company with the past usually corresponds to the expected speed of the forthcoming future. And if the future is late, then a search begins, cannot but begin, for something that could compensate for the lag of life behind ideology, for something compensating for that discomfort.

After we have learned so much about the "liberals", we can hardly doubt that they would be looking exclusively for an ideological compensation. Which ideology, then, can they have recourse to?

We are not sure if the data we have adduced would be corroborated by subsequent surveys. But if these data are not accidental, it means that our native "liberals" surpass other citizens not only in terms of the allegiance to the ideals of freedom and their sharp negation of everything which they see as something of the non-freedom character. They surpass all the rest also in another respect; in no other groups the idea of freedom stands so near in mentality to the national ethnic idea.

"Liberals" and "Non-Liberals" about the Policy of Russia in the Field of Inter-National (Inter-Ethnic) Relations (per cent)

On what should the nationality policy of Russia be oriented first of all?	"Liberals"	"Non-liberals"
On the protection of human rights irrespective of nationality	52	66
On protection of Russians in Russia	30	16
On protection of Russians residing in the Republics of the former Soviet Union	12	10
	3	3
On protection of national minorities irrespective of nationality	3	5
Finds it hard to answer		

This is how it looks like in answers to one of questions of our questionnaire.

No matter how impressive these data may be, we would not be in a hurry to classify our "Liberals" as real or potential Zhirinovsky men: they do not evince any special interest to the Liberal Democratic Party of Russia (LDPR) and its leader during the survey, and by their basic characteristics (educational standard, level of proficiency, etc.) they greatly differ from the electorate of that Party.

Nor shall we state that people from all political-ideological movements favouring liberalism are less than anybody else inclined to reckon with the fundamental liberal idea of human rights, giving preference to the rights of the representatives of a particular nation. We shall abstain from this if only because the share of those who favour the abolition of national discrimination is much greater among "liberals" than among "non-liberals", while the share of people urging to purge Russia from non-Russians is much lesser (they are quite few in the total number of the population).

Why, then, many "liberals" demand that greater attention be paid to the problems of Russians? Evidently, they are inclined to believe that it is the rights of the Russians, as compared with the rights of the peoples that are the hardest hit in the course of the reforms. But if Russian "liberals", being the most ardent supporters of the reforms now under way, begin to recall their nationality, that means that their personal interest removed to the periphery of the mentality and dissolved in much stronger striving for a "bright future" for all, begins to be voiced, that the liberal ideology alone is not enough to keep up a historical optimism. This ideology has to be supplemented by another ideology, which would be sufficiently convincing to compensate for one's inner discomfort. Another interpretation is, incidentally, possible: "liberals" feel stronger than others that their world conception is weakly rooted in Russian realities and experience a need to rely on a real force, be it reformatory authorities or, if the latter is weak, the "title nation" forming the majority of the population.

Proclivity of liberalism to the national-ethnic idea is nothing new. In its time, in Europe it asserted itself having betrothed itself exactly with the national idea. But it had to pay a high price: upheavals Europe had to pass through on that road are well known. Can we avoid them today?

We cannot say for sure that the liberal idea would look for support and assistance in the ethnic idea. To prevent the alliance of these two ideas is only possible if we succeed in skipping the version of liberalism, which initially dominated in the West, i.e., "economic" liberalism. A relatively painless, non-catastrophic development is conceivable only as a result of mastering the experience of the "social liberalism" of the twentieth century.

DRAMATIC CONFRONTATION OF DEMOCRACY AND LIBERALISM IN OLD AND NEW RUSSIA

Igor Pantin[*]

We believe we have been born to live on everything that is ready-made, that we do not have to work at all in order to reach a height, which other peoples have reached by their frantic efforts and intensive work of thought. Unfortunately, people's habits based on a kind of fatalistic hope for outside help, more than justify these strange considerations.

M. Saltykov-Shchedrin

In my view, discourse on traditions of Russian history, on the relationship between "Russian of Today" and "Russia of Yesterday" is inconceivable unless we grasp the actual divergence, and even antagonism, of democratic and liberal trends in the political history of our country. Attempts to see the reasons for this enmity are very important both for working out the strategy of the present democratization and for a new understanding of the political past of Russia.

Where do I see the pernicious effect of the confrontation of liberalism and democracy? In a nutshell, in the understanding of the genesis of the phenomena

[*] I. Pantin (D. Sc., Philos.), Professor, Editor-in-Chief of the magazine *Politicheskiye issledovaniya* (Political Studies – Polis). In Russian this article was published in the *Polis* magazine (1994, No. 3). The original text of the article has been slightly abridged.

of "democracy without freedom" (Ralf Gustaf Dahrendorf) and, respectively, freedom without democracy.

The democratic ethos, which constitutes the foundation of the democratic political system, is far from being given to the people primordially as a fact of its present existence. It is the product of a prolonged historical development in the course of which its cultural, basic values, moral aims and inner world also make progress. The character, the "code" of its behaviour, everything we call its mentality, undergoes change. What role the politics and economics play in this process is hard to anticipate. One thing is clear: the historical experience imprinted in the mentality, the habits of millions – such is an indispensable prerequisite of the formation of the democratic ethos, which, after it had taken shape, is capable of correcting in its spirit all forms of the political establishment.

At first glance, the peculiarities of the way of life and the mentality of Russians correspond to the notion of democracy: it is thinkable wherever the status of anyone is recognized as equal with the status of the rest. At any rate, the October 1917 Revolution was inspired by exactly this ideal of equality. But in practice, the equalization of the higher Estates and the Demos turned out to be the leveling of culture, convictions, habits and everyday life of Russians, giving rise to their imperial attitude to other nations. Democracy as a way of life of traditional collectives not only failed to develop into a democracy as a mode of thought and the way of government, but, on the contrary, served as a basis of an unheard-of-totalitarianism hostile to all freedom of expressing one's views opinions and interests.

I associate the historical future of liberalism, liberal values and the possibility of implanting them in the mass mentality in Russia not so much with the intrinsic history of liberal ideas and movements as with the character of Russian democracy, its genesis and the ability for self-transformation. This equally applies to the past and the present. If we somewhat simplify things we can say that if in the USA democracy practically at once got a liberal frame, if in Western Europe the confrontation of different social gives rise to a liberal-democratic complex, in Russia liberal values fully failed to fecundate a democratic ideology and mass consciousness.

"I" ENSLAVED BY "WE"

Each people itself chooses its freedoms and a form of democracy depending on the situation and the past experience, groping its own measure of relations and limitation of various freedoms. The adherents of democratic freedoms in Russia should, in addition to this, see something perfectly different: the object of their striving demands that it be conceived in a new way. As M. Gefter pointed out, history (ours and not ours) has shaped us as something much greater and much distinctive than a country, in the long run we turned out to be a peculiar continent where the motley picture of ethnoses and civilizations, ways of life, social subjects, different epochs, different levels of cultural development determined a special difference between, and at once, a special proximity of, faiths, conditions, morals, attitudes to work, property and power. But to make this difference and a simultaneous proximity "work" in behalf of forming a modern democratic ethos, it is necessary to understand one's own historical experience. The peoples of Russia should, so to say, become naturalized in a new space unfamiliar to them; to master its basic principles and see what benefits it can produce.

As we know, the type of culture is pre-set by the spiritual-value paradigm, constituting the foundation of a particular cultural community. A knew word for Russian (and partly for Russia's) culture is not the individual, as is the case in the West, but a society (community, village community, a people, etc.). If we want to determine this type of culture, we should rather call it a primitive-collectivist one, bearing in mind that "collectivism" is not synonymous of the social, being a more specific characteristic of the manifestation of the "social": the national, the political and cultural. From this definition it follows that the sources of the activity of the individual (motivations, initiatives, etc.) lie outside of him. What is predominant is, if you like, a one-way traffic from "society" (a community, an *artel*, a corporation, a collective body and a country) to the individual. Hence the passivity and subordination of the latter – he proves to be an object of social actions, a product of social development and, to a very small degree, its subject.

The predominance of culture of this kind, its reproduction on the country-wide scale is the expression not so much of society's dictates, its paternalist attitude to Man, as of the recognition by the individual himself of the natural primacy of collectivist principles, a voluntary, to one degree or another, subordination of individual interests to the social ones. Harmonization of individual and social interests is replaced here by their identification, reducing the former to an insignificant degree. It is not accidental, therefore, that the larger the share of the individual's own activity in the process of economic, political and spiritual intercourse with the world, the sharper he begins to sense the burden of the form of his relations with society, trying hard to free himself from the yoke of "collectivism".

Such an absorption of a personality by a "collective body" and, in the long run, by the state, which had struck deep roots thanks to historical vicissitudes, led in troublesome times and bloody clashes to crises and disintegration of big and small communities to which an individual belonged, and the latter, who had not been molded morally, politically or historically turned out to be unable to control the situation. To a much greater degree than state despotism, Russia in hard times was threatened by the anarchy of a multitude of individual and collective wills, which had partaken of the absence of barriers for self-assertion. Having not reached the level of self-reflection, self-control and self-limitation, the mass of the people could be driven in their actions to extremes, to the limits of the possible unless one person or an organized group managed – as a rule by coercion – to take hold of that elemental force and subjugate it, becoming a supreme judge over different strivings and interests.

Nor is the social consciousness of Russians at present a *tabula rasa* on which one may write whatever he thinks fit. Its major aspect is the so-called state-leveling consciousness (or "great power principles," "state collectivism", "We" in place of "I", etc.), which has experienced a prolonged and intricate transformation, but yet remained, in its transformed form, a factor largely determining modern social development. Substantial characteristics of this mass world outlook are as follows: man's personal dependence; the dissolution of private interests, opinions and views in "common" interests, opinions and views; rejection of the "inalienable" rights of the individual – all rights belong

to a "higher community", i.e., the state; leveling of all and sundry –
multiformity, distinctions, autonomy are impermissible, or, at least, suspicious;
intolerance – the striving to solve practically all problems by way of coercion
meted out to "minorities" in behalf of the people's Truth; suppression of
private, personal initiative only such initiatives, quests and efforts to renovate
can be displayed as are permitted by the "superiors" and which can benefit
"state interests", symbolizing "the interests of society as a whole." The leveling
etatist consciousness backed up by a totalitarian-socialist ideology has long
become the dominant of society, especially as a result of the successful
"people's" dictatorship of a single class.

Actually all the vehicles of the individual "I" in town and country were
faced with a choice: either to be destroyed physically or to renounce its own
"I", dissolving it (sincerely or insincerely) in the "We". The trend to transform
Man into a simple unit which is, subsequently, reduced to a nil (V.
Mayakovsky), according to a well-known poetic metaphor, gained in
momentum in the 1920s and, particularly, in the 1930s. Only in the end of the
1950s, partly due to the influence of the Great Patriotic War and partly due to a
new differentiation of society, a greater cultural influence of educated layers
(first of all the scientific-technological and humanitarian intelligentsia) the
massive "We" began gradually to break up. In this sense, the fate of
totalitarianism was predetermined.

LIBERALISM IN RUSSIA: CONTRADICTION IN ADJECTO

Though very important, the type of culture, the peculiarities of the psychic
of Russians are still only a canvas, on which history, especially political
history, embroiders its bizarre designs. It is hardly possible, using references to
the mass consciousness, to explain the fact that the liberal trend in Russia did
after all fail to develop into a people's movement; liberalism as an independent
factor of the power and a source of people's initiative was non-existent.

The liberals were proud of such names as Chicherin, Novgorodsev,
Kistyakovsy, Gessen and others, who were able, on a par with the European

authorities of liberalism, to advance the theory of law, especially the natural law, the study of political philosophy. But paradoxically enough, the basic political ides of European liberalism, met in Russia with a strange destiny: they were studied, shared but nobody felt the need to carry them out in practice. In 1870, Dostoyevsky wrote that "supreme liberalism" and a "supreme liberal", i.e., liberal without any aim, were possible in Russia. On the one hand, such intellectual idealism was rather the "bon ton" for persons of educated high society who did not experience the need to acquire its own political consciousness, than a *sine qua non*. The "practical liberals" from the Zemstvo movement, on the other hand, could not, in the long run, overcome the ideologem of continuing the cause of Alexander the Second-Liberator. Their timid hopes that local self-government bodies would assume general state functions did not come true till the beginning of the twentieth century. Liberals entered the revolution of 1905-1907 as a force, which just began to acquire its own, independent political identity. Despite their successes in the State Duma, they still had to work out a system of ideas, bringing it home to the mass of the people and integrate the basic strivings of Russian society, elevating them to the level of general national issues. As is known, history did not give them time to realize it.

But the main thing the Russian liberalism had failed to accomplish was to form political elites capable of relying on particular common interests and public moods in the fight against the old authorities. Rejecting the first-rate significance of the "social issue", Russian liberals permitted the populist parties together with Social-Democrats to formulate a perspective based on a radical solution of the agrarian problem, to which the majority of peasants strove and which ruled out the consensus of different ideological and social interests.

This was a starting point for further developments and new connections between political concepts and programmes. Due to the peculiar but inevitable in Russia aberration of political consciousness, the populist Parties and Bolsheviks made the doctrine of equality (imparting to it anti-bourgeois and "social" interpretation) the tool of emancipatory plans, a doctrine that could be developed into a natural law, which, in parallel with the formation of the economic theory, constituted an ideology of the fight of the bourgeoisie for a liberal society resting on liberalism, free trade and the code of civil law. Proceeding from the illusory conclusion that the social revolution, nationalization of property is the road to socialism, Bolsheviks together with Social-Revolutionaries passed to the Jacobin positions, believing that a sudden, swift and violent seizure of state power with the help of a people's rebellion is the only means of effecting profound social changes, primarily the solution of the agrarian problem.

Incidentally, Lenin and the Bolsheviks entertained another democratic principles up to 1917 – he demand that agrarian changes should be in the hands of revolutionary peasant committees. For him peasant committees signified nationalization carried out from below and, simultaneously, the departure of the mass of the people from their closed communities and the muzhiks' entrance into the "big politics." The role of the proletarian vanguard in this transformation of "Russia of slaves" into "Russia of freemen" was conceived as a tremendous one: that vanguard, Lenin believed, was destined to re-make politically and morally the vanguard part of the popular masses. Developments, however, demonstrated the Utopian character of Lenin's hopes, which he pinned on the potentialities of the proletarian vanguard – the peasants yesterday and the urban plebeians today – as well as on the ability of the masses to transform them. The democratic prospect of the "proletarian dictatorship" had proved to be a myth: it had resulted in the exclusive monopoly of Bolsheviks over political power, which later developed into a totalitarian regime, not in attracting the popular masses to the running of the state. Once again developments proved that they are determined not by the calculations and designs of leaders and the actions of Parties, but by the behavior of the mass of the rank-and-file people with their psychological make-ups, minds, superstitions, moral stereotypes and so on.

The drama of Russian political history consists, in my view, in that the democratic and liberal impulses did not supplement each other, as was the case in the USA and Western Europe.

Instead, they entered a fierce combat. The impossibility of uniting these hostile tendencies in Russia, or, at least, bringing them to mutual understanding deformed both the democratic and the liberal ideologies. Our democrats never tired of contending that liberal freedoms were superfluous, while the liberals from the "educated society" shied democratism as the main danger to freedom and the rights of the individual. As a result, democracy in Russia was assuming a plebeian, destructive character, while liberalism tended to protect itself, supporting the "rational" actions of the autocracy. *Vekhi* courageously fixed that dramatic situation, but it was not comprehended either by the "left-wingers" or the "right-wingers" and even by its own supporters.

Division into two of the single value and political space adversely affected both the democrats and the liberals. The democrats, including the Bolsheviks, had to idealize the peasantry and, subsequently, the plebeian-proletarian masses in behalf of democracy, ascribing to them in line with West European socialist canons all possible social virtues (the spirit of collectivism, revolutionary independent activity, the emancipatory mission and so on and so forth). And all this in a country where the traditionalist and tsar-abiding peasant masses were the majority hardly touched by the bourgeois civilization, where the working class of the European type was a tiny magnitude in the overall mass of the urban plebs, where the serfdom-patriarchal culture was predominant among the peasantry. The conservative denunciation of the masses, the fear of the lowest "scum" (i.e. the people proper) doomed the Russian liberals, the liberals of a new formation of the early twentieth century included, to political isolation, and their ideology – to the loss of the emancipatory aspect, to reconciliation with the autocracy and to opposition to democratic revolutionaries. As a result, a doctrine, which was in the West a striking symbol of freedom and progress, had for a long time was branded as a protective and conservative ideology. One, of course, may admire the intellectual manhood of people who refused to flirt with the dark, downtrodden masses, but in politics the unwillingness and inability to understand one's own people augurs crash.

In the context of West European history, the rupture with feudalism presupposes, as a rule, the natural development of liberalism. Such a sequence of developments sometimes seems to some people to be self-evident. Russia (and, later on, it transpired that it was not only Russia) was a clear departure from that "norm": in her social thought manifestations of radical dissatisfaction with serfdom were from the very outset overburdened by all sorts of socialist

Utopias which called in question the value of liberal freedoms. Prior to the establishment of capitalism socialism began to compete with a liberal ideology. The Russian revolutionary democrat takes as its starting point that phase of the West European situation when the idea of the natural freedom of the individual began to be ousted by the ideal of "social" liberation (as distinct from "merely" political liberation). Not the last role in the rise and development of the socially (not liberally) oriented democratic movements was played by such a premise of Russian opulist thought as "collective responsibility", "conciliarism", the rejection of the possibility of the individually possessed, atomized social freedom. History demonstrated that this premise was just as subconsciously inherent in Russian mind and the psychology of the people as was the concept of polis in the citizens of Athens or the idea of free thinking entertained by the Englishmen.

The political perspective opened up to the development of that premise proved to be exceptionally important for the future of Russian political thought – the Narodnik (Populist) movement embraced the ideas of European socialism, first anarchic, the Jacobin, in order to yield, in the long run, the initiative to the radical Social-Democrats (Bolsheviks).

Departure from the West European "norm", a radical change of the perspective testified to the fact that, despite the swift development of capitalism after 1861, no such society was formed in Russia as would be able to impart meaning to the liberal concepts of freedom as the supreme goal, the supreme rule of human intercourse, a universal ideal standing above class interests. Of course, in our country, too, liberalism developed both on the theoretical and political plane. But its dogmatic allegiance to the principles of legislative liberalism (as distinct from social liberalism) sort of confined the rebellious spirit of freedom to the rigid framework of the existing socio-political system. Even the familiarization with Marxism at the close of the 19th century did not change the state of affairs: Russian liberals proved unable to grasp the problems raised by the Narodniks and, subsequently upheld by the Bolsheviks. But it is apparent that in Russia, to a much greater degree than in any other country, freedom unaccompanied by the minimum economic and legislative (for the peasants) independence cannot exist for man – it remains a fiction simple and pure. To an equal extent, the recognition of autonomy, the self-determination of nations, private space and the freedom conscience have no actual value, if it is not accompanied by the fight against the autocracy – the main force of the political oppression of society.

It was precisely in the name of freedom and the provision of real freedom for the majority of the Russian population, and not only for the educated, rationally thinking minority, that Russian liberals should have demanded an end to the Estate privileges and the measures to free economically the peasants from serfdom. Only on this condition could they have radically strengthened the traditions of European liberalism on Russian soil, fulfilling their progressive function of coping with their historical task thanks to their inner aspirations and inspiring principles. Russian liberalism, however, failed to grasp the requirements of progress. Liberalism in Russia lacked much that was essential to become an organized political force, and still less, to win a massive support. But the main thing, perhaps, was the circumstance that in conditions of a peasant country, which had just begun to pass to capitalism, the general issue of liberalism – "the freedom of the individual" – could not turn into a focal point of political life.

THAT ODD MODERNIZATION...

Speaking generally and confining myself to mere abstraction, I would define the situation with democracy and liberalism in Russia as a manifestation of the rather antinomian nature of its historical development. Russia was a country where the Western tradition of high culture was not only accepted, but also developed thanks to the creative endeavours of the coriphaeuses of literature, music and science. But at the same time Russia was the most backward European country in terms of the number of schools, public health and welfare establishments, a country where poverty and material hardships made people unreceptive to the riches of their own culture, let alone the world culture, to universal human ideas of good, freedom and civility.

After 1861, part of society took the road of Western economic development. Large-scale industry was being established (with the help of the Government), railway roads were built, output of coal, petroleum and iron ore increased rapidly. But the industrial revolution in town had not been supplemented by a social revolution in the countryside. On the contrary, it gave rise to the "quasi-traditional" form of economy – the system of semi-feudal serfdom.

At least, the educated society of Russia began to move, step by step, in the direction of the liberal political culture of the West. But the liberals' mistrust of democracy reinforced by the wholesale terrorism on the part of the "People's Will" and the assassination of Alexander the Second led them to the deadlock. The radicalism of liberal people turned out to be conformism: expressing the best that there was in Russian culture – civil courage, thirst for the truth, vigilant conscience, the individual's striving for freedom – radicalism failed to cope with its historical tasks, primarily with the solution of the peasant problem.

At the end of the 19th century and the beginning of the 20th century, the principles and ideals of liberalism did not grow obsolete, they just had to change their form, entering into a dialogue with the "pre-history" of society and the latest trends of its development if they claimed seriously to become a liberal alternative of unity of the culturally split society. At first glance, the Narodniks and Social Democrats (the Bolsheviks) with their social collectivist programmes represented a democratic alternative to liberals. But in practice the opposite took place: orienting themselves on the revolutionary activity of the plebeian peasant masses they had to retreat from democracy under the impact of developments. Democracy as a system of values and democracy as a mechanism of government had departed from each other for a long time. The people's spontaneity transcended in 1917-1920 the framework of the solution of social problems, engulfing cities and towns, barbarizing the life of millions upon millions and calling in question not only bourgeois civilization, but also civilization at large. During the "Russian year 1793" the Bolsheviks had to save society, "bourgeois" culture, not democracy and freedom, doing this with the help of dictatorial methods. In conditions of the Civil War the treatment of freedom as a value has dramatically vanished, largely predetermining the triumph of totalitarianism. The country concerned with material problems, by the ardent desire "to have" in place of wise dictum "to be" fell victim to the ambitious plans of industrialization, wholesale unification, standardization of production and consumption which were presented as the programme of modernization.

The antinomian nature of the historical development of Russia is explained theoretically in the concept of the "catching-up development" or the "catching-up modernization". It stands to reason that this concept in working of which I, too, took part in the mid-1980s is not the key to all the problems of our native history. Yet it lays emphasis on factors which are very essential to be able to understand our past – the efforts to straighten Russia's road, to borrow from Western Europe technological innovations not only helped advance our country, but, under certain circumstances, resulted in disintegrating and destructive consequences.

The need *to catch up with the West* dictated a special method of modernization. As distinct from European countries, large-scale reforms in the social system of Russia were largely carried out at the initiative of the autocratic state power, which imposed changes both on the people, and on the ruling quarters. Such was the case, for instance, with the reforms of Peter the Great, and the abolition of serfdom in 1861. This is not the place to analyze the genesis of that phenomenon. I shall only point out that this "upside-down" pattern of development when the role of the subject of reforms was played by autocratic authorities was conditioned by the weakness, underdevelopment of social forces interested, due to their position, in changes, the forced, non-voluntary character of the reforms being carried out (sometimes under the threat of a catastrophe), and, lastly, to the political apathy of the basic mass of the population, especially at the outset of the transformations.

Such a pattern of development, as the historical experience of Russia and some other countries demonstrates, is far from being optimal; what is more, it is associated with serious dangers and contradictions. First, under this pattern of modernization, the political subjects of transformations really interested in them are formed slowly with difficulty. The elements of social structure essential to support the changes exist in embryonic form, while the ideology, more often than not, is of a contemplative, Utopian character, refusing to come forward in order to pose and solve major problems of the country's development. Secondly, in the absence of political opposition to the initiatives of the "top layers" (if that opposition does appear, it is immediately suppressed), the impulses from "below" acquire, as they grow stronger, a negative, destructive tendency. In conditions of a nation-wide crisis and the weakness of power (as was the case in 1917) the energy of lower layers leads to a social explosion and chaos. Thirdly, modernization by way of "a revolution from above" leaves out of account the social and cultural specificity of the country, treating it as something to be abolished as an anarchronism. The "Western" elements being introduced destroy the systems integrity of civilization that has taken shape, deforming it and giving rise to new and more numerous problems than before.

ANTI-LIBERAL DEVIATION OF NATIVE DEMOCRACY

The democratic movement in Russia was based on the movement of "lower classes" – the peasantry and the urban workers. Correspondingly, the ideology of groups and parties representing those classes was more of the social and economic character than of the political one. It was only on border-line between the 70s and the 80s of the 19th century that the political content of Russian democratism manifested itself more or less clearly in the phenomenon of the "People's Will" movement. Later it was superseded by Bolshevism, which, incidentally, did not change the predominantly social orientation of Populism. Russian democrats, Narodniks (Populists) or Bolsheviks were all equally interested primarily in the economic revolution which would open us possibilities for political and other changes, not in the legislation or a mechanism which could provide the citizens with a free choice, in particular in the economic sphere. Here I come very closely to the explanation of the first and, perhaps, main distinctive features of Russian democracy – its complete indifference to the form of the future state system so far as it expresses "the interests of the people."

The Russian problem is largely the problem of economic, rather than political liberation. Without freeing the popular masses economically one could create a free individual. But, perhaps, in no other country of the world, the specifically economic interpretation of social life was developed so strongly as in Russia. Hoping that it would be possible to revive the immense people through a radical revolution in relation to property, the Narodniks and even more so the Bolsheviks practically omitted from their concepts moral and political factors capable of influencing the course of historical development, and sometimes even determining it. That is the reason why democracy in Russia, which rejected "bourgeois freedoms" and rebuked all reforms, was so inefficient in working out moral values, the rights of the individual, the responsibilities of the state, etc. All privacy, self-perfection were identified with the suspicious "bourgeois individualism", with the allegedly anti-historical values of "abstract humanism". The aspirations of the individual, private life, unlikeness with others were all – from the standpoint of the demands of the economics – something dubious, false, incompatible with the activities in behalf of the future. A social revolution presupposed sacrifice of prosperity, happiness and even people's life and the Russian Bolsheviks of the heroic period demanded such sacrifices from themselves and their followers.

But such black-and-white vision of the present and the future was fraught with danger. The state operating on behalf of the people and its interests was the single and immutable framework of relations, the single reality authentic ontologically and primary morally.

On the one hand, such a state stood in no need to define itself (a republic, the parliament, independent courts, etc.), on the other, the protection of the individual from the state in case of the conflict of their interests was in advance declared a pseudo-problem. There can be no conflict between fiction and reality. The painful problem of the ethic choice between the state and Man was *a priori* solved in favour of the state. But in so doing, democratism threw the doors open to totalitarianism: the activity of the state in the economic and social spheres was everything, while the values of a pluralistic society were nothing.

All that was individual, human and personal could be tolerated only in case it was immediately directed to the common welfare.

We still have to grasp fully this one-sided dialectics of Russian democracy (socialism) and totalitarianism. So far I shall confine myself to one premise: not liberated internally, not having a strong feeling of personal dignity as well as the feeling of responsibility, the Russian man in the street treated liberation as an anarchy which can only be bridled by a strong state. Various manifestations of freedom are not merely coordinated or regulated, they are suppressed as something running counter to the interests of the people, hostile to it. In contradistinction to what John Stuart Mill said, a Russian sharing the values of democracy (and, respectively, a politician) could have said: "The state knows what Man needs better than any individual."

A dual meaning could be discerned in the fact that Russian democratic thought assumed the form of socialist "common welfare" – a peculiar democratic Utopia. On the one hand, it implied a transition to a more radical form of democratic world outlook, a means of entrenching oneself at the given position with the help of the "latest word" of the European social theory. On the other, it is a proof of the rupture between the given thought and the specific national problems of Russia, the overestimation of the level of development reached by the popular masses.

In this way, the democratic content of the ideology of Narodniks and Social Democrats cannot be rejected. It was expressed first and foremost in the realization of the need to liberate the "lower classes" from oppression, which was largely based on economic relations. But democracy as machinery of government was not even posed as a problem. For the political programme of democrats boiled down to the need "to destroy as far as possible the domination of the upper classes over the lower ones in the state system", while they were "practically indifferent" to choosing the way of achieving this. The democrat will not stop at "carrying out reforms by material enforcement," he is "prepared to sacrifice the freedom of speech and constitutional forms for the sake of reforms" (N. Chernyshevsky).

Obviously, such an understanding of democracy looks vague and limited from the standpoint of notions about modern democracy. And it is actually such, since the main prerequisites for working out new European concepts of democracy were simply lacking in pre-revolutionary Russia. A socialist due to his totality of views and convictions borrowed from the study of the science and the political experience of Europe, a democrat due to his faith in the historical righteousness of the people, to his compassion for, and active participation in, the cause of humiliated and disinherited, the Russian intellectual had always sided with "the people" *opposing* higher Estates, i.e. the minority. Unlike the socialist doctrine, his perception of democratic values and ideals was in an embryonic state. But we should bear in mind that the fight for that peculiar, historically limited ideal of democracy constituted an essential element of social transformations in Russia and a condition of her advance (though not immediate but through the nightmarish totalitarianism) to the new, European frontiers.

The distinctive feature of Russian democracy consists in that it had been formed *prior* to the emergence of a massive democratic movement in the country and *independently* of it it had been formed as the result of the influence of the theory and practice of the democratic and labour movement in the West on the radical contingent of the intellectual commoners.

Generally speaking, the Russian peasantry, which was socially stratified and traditionalist by its mentality and psychology, could not serve as a basis for a really democratic movement in the country. The elemental forces inherent in Pugachev's rebellion were observed in all peasant actions up to 1917. Ages of slavery had succeeded: the majority of the population lacked the deep feelings of their independence and responsibility. And if the democratic movement did exist in Russian society, this was largely due to the specific position, psychology of the "educated Estates", their extraordinary responsiveness to people's sufferings, due to an intensive quest for a "formula of progress" which would take into account the needs of the majority.

Substantial difference in the culture of the "educated Estates", on the one hand, and that of the popular masses, on the other, gave birth to formidable difficulties facing the democracy-minded intelligentsia. As no other layer of Russian society, the given part of the educated people felt deeply the injustice of the state of affairs in the country, taking to heart closest of all the hardships of the peasants, the laymen generally. But intellectuals failed to penetrate this environment alien to them, to see its motivations, goals and values – the people's masses were downtrodden by the burden of poverty, ignorance, and prejudices which put up practically insurmountable barrier between the "master" (no matter what he was) and the muzhik.

In Russian conditions to be a democrat is immeasurable more than simply to recognize the sovereignty of the people: one had to perform Copernicus-like revolution in one's own world conception, adopting the viewpoint of the cultural elite, connected with Russia, with the problems of people's life, using the Western ideological tradition. One can readily understand the enthusiasm Plekhanov, a newly-converted Marxist, when he began to see, thanks to "scientific socialism", the significance of the working class whose mission it was to bring the revolutionary ideas home to the peasantry. For the first time, he hoped, the ideas of social liberation would cease to be the property of a narrow circle of intellectuals, acquiring a truly popular strength. Incidentally, these hopes were only partly realized: the "Russian workers" in the person of Bolsheviks did manage to lead the revolution, but they failed to purge the peasantry of its patriarchal mentality, prejudices, habits and routine. The feedback impact of those who were led on those who were in the lead, i.e., the masses on the elite, was so strong that the advanced industrial workers were literally dissolved in the conservative and inert mass of the philistines.

THE MEANING OF DEMOCRACY LOST

The historical notion of "democracy" has long been opposed to the notion of "individualism" not only in Russia, but it is only with us that the "defenders of the people", the "representatives of the masses" can demagogically treat the specific and formal freedoms and rights of the individual as something having no bearing on the essential "people's interests", being secondary and alien to them. The predominance in the mass mentality of such notions of democracy creates soil for the "tyranny of the majority" (Alexis Tocqueville), for the populist illusions, not to speak of the fact that in the 1920s and the 1930s it provided a demagogue with a chance of becoming a dictator and a despot. One can, of course, call the notions of Russians about the rights of the individual and democracy ochlocratic, but this gives little to solve the enigma of the Russian sphinx, since the very prejudices of Russian democracy, their sources, nature and consequences remain outside the object of the analysis. But the time of such "democratism" seems to have passed. One of the major tasks of the contemporary period is, in my view, the need to bridge the gap between the "popular" and the "democratic" so as to impart to the "popular" in Russia a truly democratic sense.

And here I am coming to the third distinctive feature of Russian democracy.

Behind the inability to treasure personal freedom and civil rights was concealed not only the poverty, conservatism and prejudices of the people, but also a sort of "rational" factors, in particular the people's attitude to the state as the supreme instance empowered to trample under foot the interests of the individual, society's primacy over the individual, the primacy of the "people" over the "cultured classes. It is these features that unite to form a specific "populist complex" of Russian democracy persisting to this date.

Among the past traditions, which can be traced in the last two ages of Russia up to the present day and which transform the ideas of democracy, the first place, I believe, goes to the Russians' specific understanding of the "people". In Russia with her weak development of modern social relations and a relatively insignificant, in terms of its influence on the masses, higher cultured layer, with hypertrophied bureaucratic apparatus, the notion of the "people" embraces not the bulk of the population, but primarily (and sometimes, even exceptionally), its lower layers. Intellectuals, entrepreneurs (urban and rural) and, of course, officials were considered to be outside the notion of the "people". In this rigid opposition, the notion of the "people" was first accepted and rationalized by populist intellectuals, and, subsequently, by the Bolsheviks. A sort of a "populist, Narodnik complex" of mentality had struck root, when a higher and more developed and cultured layer of the nation feels, at least on the level of world outlook, its secondary role in relation to the "popular" soil, on the one hand, and in relation to the state, on the other. The significance of cultural values is belittled, being sort of subject to "moral doubts" (Berdyaev). The supreme truth is sought in the life of the people regarded as solely organic and meaningful, not in the ideals of freedom, culture and its achievements. With such an attitude to culture, the intelligentsia is practically unable to discharge its true cultural mission.

Further on, Russian "collectivism" and Russian "conciliarism" were for a long time praised as the advantage of the Russian people. But in actual fact that signified inability of an individual man to live in spiritual autonomy, intolerance of those who think differently, the quest for the "truth" not inside but outside of oneself. A developed personality was deprived of the right to uphold his own truth or have a more complex, individualized mentality, feeling himself an organic component of the people. Not only was he deprived of this, he was also denied the possibility of using his individuality and talent so as to realize his predestination to be more the "people", than the laymen (Berdyaev). Of course, today when the majority of the population of Russia have acquired certain experience, have become more educated, gaining access to TV and radio broadcasts, to newspapers and books, the "populist complex" of democracy has become extremely threadbare, but its survivals are still strong. And this is seen in the violent resistance put up to liberal ideas today.

In conditions of the non-liberal society, it was quite natural that Russian democrats should consider as the main problem of political life the rule by the majority, i.e., the democracy of the majority. But it was not the classical liberal problem of combining the rule of the majority with respect for the rights of the minority. Nay, according to the Russian democratic tradition the majority was primordially in the right, since it was the majority: the only question could only be of overcoming the barriers in the way of winning "the sovereignty of the people". Even sharing the apprehensions of the "cultured society" as regards the barbarism, underdevelopment and the prejudices of the majority, Russian democrats firmly believed that the interests and rights of the "people" are sacred and all that has to be done was to implement them in life by all means, fair or foul.

Evidently, the sad experience of Russia shows that the mass of the population, which is equal in poverty and hardships, though living in different economic conditions, ethnically heterogeneous and stratified socially, with multiformity of ways of life and interests, is incapable of independently representing itself, promoting its interests on its own behalf. Its decisive political influence on the state of affairs in the country consists in its support of a "strong" power, which stands above society and acts as a guardian of its interests. A "strong", paternalistically programmed state, no matter how it calls itself, forms a political foundation for the intervention of authorities in all public affairs, as well as for the rule of numberless bureaucrats in the name of the "people". In conditions of the underdevelopment of civil society and hypertrophied centrism, the ideology of democratism with its priority of nation-wide requirements and the ethics of the "common welfare", could not predetermine anything. It could only express the *striving* to solve elementary problems relating to the majority, but the *method* of actions and the means resorted to be dictated by the circumstances. And it is the character of actions and the means employed that constitute the real content of democracy.

PROSPECTS OF YESTERDAY OR THE FUTURE?

To sum up, the impossibility of solving in a democratic way (i.e., with the help of compromises) the problems raised by capitalist modernization determined the polarization of the Russian liberation movement into a non-liberal (later anti-liberal) democracy and non-democratic liberalism. Their confrontation was reinforced by the circumstance that at each critical political juncture the democratic elements were inclined to adopt revolutionary methods of struggle (revolutionarism), while liberalism tended to compromise with the monarchy, sacrificing the idea of sovereignty of the people. The inclinations of the former were reproduced in a Freudian way in the lexicon: Perestroika was at once called a "revolution"). The October Revolution, of course, signified the beginning of deep economic and social reforms, which were so essential for Russia' progress. But simultaneously it revealed something essentially different – the real political content of the plebeian-peasant democracy as the structure of the rule of the totalitarian elites. The dictatorial regime of new modernizers vindicated that monopoly of power by their "popular" policy it allegedly pursued, by the ideology of "social justice". However, the acceptance by the majority of the population of the basic principles of the system of new society was secured through the suppression of political rights and civil liberties, relentless repressions against all non-conformists.

And yet, returning to the past of Russia in explaining her totalitarian-socialist road, I would not exaggerate the role of coercive methods in asserting post-revolutionary political and social system. For arbitrariness, disbelief in the force of right, laws have literally pervaded the souls of Russians. (Chernyshevsky wrote that each of us, every Russian is a Napoleon or, more exactly, Khan Batu). The revolution gave an outlet to this non-liberal, non-democratic elemental force of the people's character, sanctioning it morally, setting it tasks and providing it with the means to accomplish them. The post-revolutionary Stalinist regime turned these abuses into a system of government policy and sanctioned them with the doctrine of "growing class struggle" as socialism won its successes. As an ideology and a political movement it had managed to base itself on the basic traits of the *national character* of Russians dating back to the past.

In all its hypostases, freedom begins with the re-making of Man. Russians, in my opinion, have not yet risen to the level of perceiving their lives as everyday struggle and mission, understanding freedom as their moral duty, seeing their own frontiers and the frontiers of others. They still pin their greatest hopes on the state, not on themselves. But we should give them their due: in recent years they learn fast. Though contradictory and dramatically, but the realization of personal freedom does arise in the broad layers of the Russian people. The realization is growing of the close interdependence of freedom, progress and social justice. For the first time in the history of Russia the demand for the rights of the individual and for the principle of local self-government turns into an issue for the people, not for the nomenclature, the powers that be. It may be that it would be precisely Russia that would form a political community in the confines of a single state not as a unified world, but as a "World of worlds" (Gefter), realizing a new understanding of freedom. According to him, free is a society, where all the traditions have equal rights and an equal access to the centres of power (Feierabend), as distinct from a customary definition of freedom whereby the individuals have equal rights to achieve respective positions. At long last, the realization is growing that the basic forms of independence require the rule of law and so on and so forth.

And yet, the decisive point in radicalizing the simple formulas of freedom and human rights in Russia – the main prerequisite of the crisis-free entry of Russia into the twenty-first century – is the practical surmounting of the survivals of totalitarianism in the political and social life of the country. Our liberal mentality has too long lingered at the polemic, anti-Communist stage, while the drafting of a constructive programme of the fight against all kinds of last vestiges of totalitarianism and autocracy was postponed, if not generally curtailed because of the economic crisis. Meanwhile, a prolonged and painstaking cultural work has to be done by all the component parts of our society, primarily by us ourselves if the idea of freedom is to become part and parcel of Russian mentality. Much has to be reorganized in the state, bequeathed to us. But first of all we have to assert firmly the liberal method of political struggle (the liberal ethos), which all social forces should unfailingly apply.

Russia today is at a crossroads: in her social and political life the culture of harmonizing positions, compromises and quest for accord will be either asserted or a past tradition would gain the upper hand, according to which the opponents should be by all means defeated, destroyed and discarded once and for all. The first alternative can, though not immediately, raise us to the level of problems of the early twenty-first century, while the second one can hurl us back, to the degeneration of social practice, to the customary system of supremacy and subordination. It would be absurd to subdivide these trends as the "market" and the "non-market", "reformatory" or "non-reformatory" ones. What is at issue is a different thing: would the liberalism borrowed from the West in its "economized" form be able to give an impetus to the search for a broader space for Russian freedom.

LEFT MOVEMENTS IN
POST-AUTHORITARIAN SOCIETY

Kiva Maidanik[*]

"Left" or "traditionally left" imply in these notes ideological and political movements, tendencies, culture, attitudes, symbols, traditions, etc. which typically represent the interests of labour (contrary to those of property); of bottom strata (contrary to the power of the top strata, i.e. the dominating minority); the ideology of collectivism, solidarity, equality, internationalism and democracy.

This category, born by the developing industrial civilization and the corresponding ideological and political classification of society are not eternally unchangeable. But despite its mishaps during Perestroika and post-Perestroika in Russia, it will surely retain its significance in Europe, Latin America and partly in the regions of Asia and Africa.

I would like to emphasize from the very beginning that the author does not separate himself from the left culture and all critique to that effect is at the same time self-criticism...

The weakness of the left sector of civil society or, rather, its weakening, the relative or absolute marginalization of left movements, the crisis of their

* K. Maidanik, Cand. Sc. (Hist.), leading researcher of the Institute of World Economics and International Relations, RAS. This article was published in Russian in *Svobodnaya mysl*, No. 9, 1994.

ideology and organizations appear to be one of the most evident and all-round tendencies of the world political development of the 1980s. This also refers to societies which live up through the crisis of industrial and national capitalism (and technogenic civilization) and the majority of the Third World countries that pay for the structural and civilization transition in the West (and the disintegration of the "East") but often gain from its consequences in the political aspect (democratization). This also refers to societies of "World No. 2" which are now becoming democratic – at least till the summer of 1993. Since we are speaking about the situation of the collapsing authoritarian regimes, the political defeat of the left appears to reside even in the stability of their influence, at least in the countries of the South. For about two hundred years (from about 1789 to 1981) similar situations inevitably marked the period of their formation and the success of the left forces, the maximum efficiency of their historical action – revolutionary, reformatory, cultural and ideological. This took place even in those cases when their political struggle did not lead directly to the victory (1848-1951). Today fingers can count the countries, which reproduce this political tendency of former structural crisis (within the framework of the industrial civilization cycle). First of all, they are Brazil and South Africa, and, to some extent, Uruguay and Salvador, and maybe Mexico. The rise in the influence of the left-off-centre forces in a number of East-European countries in 1993-1994 reflects a different tendency which does not have direct analogy in history (see below).

In any case Russia is no exception in that respect. This was too evident till October 1993, and, it seems, the developments that followed did not bring qualitative shifts.

It is true that one can compare the influence of the forces that put forth left or partly left programmes only with respect to the first decade that followed the October 1917 Revolution. Then political society was devoured by the state and we cannot speak about the degree of influence of the left within the framework of a new community (with respect to 99.9 per cent of the voters), at least it will be quite difficult, given no sociological surveys. If one compares with the situation of 70-75 years long, he can easily notice that the current political influence of the left is three to seven times lower than at that time (take into account the 75 per cent of votes the left received in the election to the Constituent Assembly and the victory of the "red" in the Civil War) and their ability to influence the course of history decreased by an order or two.

Today's polls of public opinion are an indirect indicator of this phenomenon while the direct indicator is the results of the elections, even the most favourable for the Russian left (December 12, 1993).

The two left parties collected less than 21 per cent of votes. Add to that number the votes for the left-off-centre candidates and we will get in any case more than 25 per cent. But we are talking about 56 (officially) or 46 per cent (using other data) of the grown-up population. In other words, the real influence of the "left sector" does not exceed 15-16 per cent. These calculations correlate with other data. Only 6 to 7 per cent of the former members of the CPSU renewed their membership in the "parties-successors", separated from the state. The majority of the intelligentsia is militantly anti-communist, especially "the creative" intelligentsia. The influence of the left ideas and values can hardly be detected among the youth and it is minimal in the working strata. The major part of the population continues to support the right wing, militantly anti-communist (in the modern, non-Islamic world) leadership of the country. Today the major part of the President's supporters is actively anti-socialist.

The left movement is fragmented in terms of ideology and organization: it did not come to its senses after the collapse of the quasi-left regime and the left-off-centre tendencies of 1988-1991; the major part of it ("traditionalists") did not learn a real lesson from what had happened while the considerable part (national communists) embarked upon the road of ideological and political revision of former values which in fact drive it beyond the values, standards and ideology of the left movement. The new democratic left, the "left of the end of the century", are represented by a score of groups, trends and parties whose aggregate political weight is several times smaller than the influence of the left forces in modern Mexico and Venezuela, Nicaragua and Spain.

From the first glance, the causes of this situation are quite evident: the historical memory of the GULAG and Prague in 1968, repressions and prohibitions in the name and for the sake of socialism and communism, under the banners of "Marxism-Leninism" and so on. Add to this the economic incapability of the state, quasi-left model which manifested itself when the tasks of industrialization were completed against the background of the economic breakthroughs in the world, and the inability to reform this model in an evolutionary way which was identified in the period of Perestroika, let alone the inability to self-development. All this multiplied by the decisive anti-bureaucratic complex of mass consciousness, which appears in the situation of impotence of the left, and the left reformatory leadership was transformed by the right liberal trend into anti-communist. Add the bankruptcy of the left in working out the socialist alternative of statehood, the putsch in August 1991, and the period that followed when all ex-communist leadership deserted to the camp of the victors, the stand of the "intellectual leaders" and mass media and some other circumstances which we shall discuss later. All this is our own. But there are global things: the mighty demonstration (and later imitation, too) effect, especially on the youth, like in the countries of Eastern Europe in 1990.

As a result, the right liberals led the process of changes with their system of values and anti-values. The left-values are then regarded as a force, which embodies the past...

Nevertheless, it seems to me that all this does not explain the current development in full measure and is not enough to foretell the future.

What are the causes that made the left retreat simultaneously in so different situations like Russia and Latin America, Eastern Asia and Western Europe? Why has the phenomenon of 1944-1947 failed to repeat in today's Latin America and the Third World in general where the majority of defeated authoritarian regimes were right wing and the left were an anti-dictator, democratic force? There is no need to explain the latter by the effect of "developments in the East": similar tendencies manifested themselves south of Rio Grande before the Perestroika events although later the "collapse in the East" had an evident effect on the processes in the South.

Why were the developments in Russia, contrary to those in Poland, Hungary, Lithuania, the Ukraine, Byelorussia and Bulgaria, not cushioned by the "post-communist" processes of 1991-1993 – the retreat of the left to the opposition and the heaviest economic, social, political, cultural and psychological mishaps which results from the two-year rule of the right? What are the prospects of the left, in the light of the above, in Russia against the background of what is going on in Central Europe and the Third World?

Possibly the *collapse* (defeat, retreat) of authoritarian regimes and the all-round weakening of the left forces (both authoritarian and democratic) in 1983-1993 are motivated not only by the processes of national history but also by some global laws. Otherwise, we cannot approach the fact of "simultaneous and unidirectional" tendencies.

It seems that the essence of the problem (and one of the major difficulties) resides in the situation of overlapping and interaction of two structural crises, the end of two cycles, so typical of the 1980s-1990s.

On the one hand, this is a regular, second crisis of the "long wave", the so-called "Kondratyev-4" crisis, which changes the technico-economic paradigm of development in the centre of the system, affects all levels and spheres, domestic and foreign relations of "late industrial capitalism", and crystallizes a new system of structures. From this point of view, the on-going processes can be compared with those that went in the 1930s-1950s.

On the other, what is evident is the crisis of industrial (and "national") civilizations which covers not only the past Kondratyev cycle (1930s-1980s) but also the three cycles that preceded. This crisis struck a number of important structures – political, social, cultural, ideological – which underwent radical changes, being sort of inherited from the early industrial system of structures – through the capitalism of "coal" and "steel" to the capitalism (and the world system) of "oil and automobile" the "new scientific and technical revolution and TNC's expansion".

The essence of the problem under review consists in that of all trends (sectors) of the ideological and political range of modern societies the left trends with their similarity, ideological attitudes and political culture turned to be most vulnerable to the both crises – the one which was brought about by the transition to the "microchip paradigm" an that which carried a civilization shift. They hit all left trends – revolutionary and reformatory, Marxism and other ideologies, those that were in office and in opposition, and those whose formulae and values were used to ideologically legitimatize the "total community", according to M. Cheshkov.

Almost all "corner stones" of being and consciousness, all historical processes that gave life and identity to the left trends, were affected.

Here is the chronological list:

– struggle against monarchies, oligarchies, dictatorship (later fascism, too), for political freedoms and democracy;

– social struggle of the "lower strata" against "top strata", of those exploited against the property owners and the authorities for the radical or partial redistribution;

– the struggle of the oppressed nations against colonialism and traditional neocolonialism for independence and equality;

– the growing role of the state – the major subject which redistributes the wealth and power in favour of the majority; consolidation of the sovereignty and economic development;

– permanent presence of ideological systems, political parties in society's culture; the major importance of these factors in social development;

– the mystic (Utopia?) of a new, just and rational world, the "new man" and new age which can be attained in the historically shortest time – primarily through a political revolution that embodies all the commandments and processes of collective liberation about which we talked above. (In the 20th century for the part of the left the role of a major vehicle in progress and liberation was to be played by the cycles of large-scale reforms.)

Many of these factors continue to act today in full measure in the countries of the traditional and new Third World. Nevertheless, it seems that, guided by these factors alone and resting only on those political and ideological constructs we talked about above, the left will not be able to play the historical role they used to do.

Authoritarian and dictatorial regimes retreat and fall down all over the globe. This time in the majority of cases this happens not so much under the pressure of the forces, led by the left, as because of the pressure of the new economic factors and owing to the political stand of the centrist (Third World) and/or right-wing (Central and Eastern Europe) forces. The movement slogans, calling for the struggle for individual freedom, became all around a cornerstone of the anti-left (not only anti-communist) policy and ideology.

The role of the traditional class struggle (proletariat against domestic bourgeoisie) as a factor which constitutes the anti-capitalist left continues to diminish even in those regions where it was decisive (Western Europe, Japan, the countries of the South Cone).

The anti-colonial struggle has completed and the new international situation – both economic and political – leave no prospect for the traditionally left, "anti-imperialist" variants of modernization, the struggle for development and equality.

Simultaneously, the "secular" nationalism of any kind, which in its anti-imperialist version became in the 1950s-1970s the major political and ideological vector of development and consolidation of the left in the Third World found itself under strong pressure. And it is not only from the "new economy" but also from nationalism (Asia and Africa), ethnic and religious fundamentalism and other ideological tends and tendencies which can hardly be "assimilated" organically by the left political culture.

The role of the omnipresent and/or almighty state – the principal tool of progress, social and national protection – is disputed in the new situation by both those from the top and bottom (the anti-bureaucratic and anti-corruption syndrome of civil society) and is put to doubt by new imperatives of the economic development and impulses coming from the cultural and psychological sphere.

Meanwhile, in all three worlds of humanity the left (except anarchists) has fought for the expansion of the state in the economic, social (and political and cultural in the East and South) spheres and implemented that when in office. It is quite righteous that now the left pays for that by retreating together with the state.

Similarly, ideologies undergo such mishaps even in greater measure. This refers to all ideologies but this process for the left turned to be most painful primarily because the role of the integral ideological system in their political culture, identity and the "calling" was greater than in other sectors of the ideological and political range. Let alone the fact that this role was decisive, integrating and legitimatizing for the communist trend of the left. It is particularly in this case that we speak about the collapse of the ideological construction (dogmatic Marxism) which turned to be the payment for its ossification for half a century and the unnatural "cohabitation" with the state.

The same may be said about the going decay of the role of political parties – in past the major entities of left ideology and the left movement in the "first" (except the USA) and the "second" worlds.

These two worlds cast into oblivion the mystic of the world's "radical and fast transformation" by way of political action, an uprising and liberation of the masses and through the revolutionary state activity. This process is clearly felt in the Third World, too. The revolution's romantic humanism is retreating step by step to the background, both in ideological terms and in secular mass consciousness, yielding to new realities: nuclear threat, the price and effectiveness of revolutions, the new status of the market as a vehicle and regulator of development, especially post-industrial.

This kind of market perception, the necessity of "denationalization", the processes of cultural and psychological individualization and the attending circumstances of the global (civilization) transition have never been among the values and ideals of the left for they were alien to their traditional political culture.

Such are the most important directions of influence of the structural and civilization shifts on the present (and future?) of the left forces at the end of the century.

Evidently, practically each of the factors cited was effective in the USSR because of the generic features of the state regime and due to its individual features (duration; the totalitarian character of the structure ties which excludes the very existence of the left in civil society; the influence of the ethnic factor, etc.).

At the historical crossroads of 1987-1991 the decisive role was played by the historical ties of the left with the former system (in Central and Eastern Europe) and its ideology – state, anti-democratic, "class", anti-market and geopolitical.

This, combined with the factors and commandments of the global order we talked about and which embodied not for the sake of demonstration resulted in that the popular anti-authoritarian revolutions in the majority of Central

European countries and their analogous in the Baltic republics and in Moscow (Leningrad) turned to be headed (at once or in several months) by the block of centrist and right (anti-socialist, liberal) forces with the priority of the latter.

The left retained certain influence in those countries in which they were supported by strong social and national tradition (Czechoslovakia, the GDR, Bulgaria). In those countries where they were mainly regarded as a force which was alien to the country's independence or in the countries where anti-communism became the ideology of both the state and civil society, even emerging (Russia), they found themselves on the periphery.

However, why the situation did not change in Russia over the first two years of the administration by the right wing? The results of their administration, especially in the social, political and criminal spheres, are such that, given a different national or historical situation, the forces, opposing the government, would have changed such a government as it happened in Lithuania, Poland, Hungary and will possibly happen in several other countries of South-Eastern Europe.

We have talked about the objective factors of the situation – economic, psychological, "traditionalist", those of generation and inertia (when the current authorities are regarded as yesterday's fighters against the former state bureaucratic hierarchy) – which together with the monopoly of mass media allow to partly neutralize the effect of the "three year results" and used for two-odd years the anti-communist syndrome like a magnetic field to hold plasma. But that is a different matter.

I should emphasize here that a good deal of responsibility for the weakness of the left forces belongs to their and our own sins after the August developments.

Let us recall them in the order of their importance.

– The cowardice, impotence and mass defection of yesterday's top left in August-September, 1991 – and later at the end of the year (the voting in the Supreme Soviet of Russia for the programme of shock therapy and for Belovezhskoye agreement that disintegrated the USSR). Nothing of the kind has ever happened in Central Europe. It seems that we too have an evident proof of the historical bankruptcy of the "left" elite and the left idea. Especially compared with their historical predecessors.

– Having appeared in the parliament and bodies of the local power, in the economic structures, the "communists" are still regarded as part of the authorities with all their sins and their own share of responsibility for the economic, anti-social and criminal disorder in the country.

– The major part of the communists which remained loyal to the CPSU or the Communist Party of the Russian Federation failed to overcome their old dogmas and did not learn from what had happened. This also refers to the major part of leadership of the "traditional left". The reason for this phenomenon is multifarious (given the decisive role of the "generation" and "Gorbachev" factors) but the very reality is quite obvious in their non-democratic and anti-market orientation.

It seems, however, that such dogmatism of all-round defense is no worse than that which was going on with the traditional "ideological" (communist) left. The other part of its leadership began to search for the way out of the situation on the lines of nationalistic revision of the former ideological maxims, having allied with the "white", "red-and-brown" (Stalinist trend) and, in certain moments, with "brown" trends of the opposition.

Such an evolution is not merely a reaction of the man that is drowning and is ready to catch for the straw. First of all, all these groups are related by a "national state" idea and from that point nationalism really seems to be a concluding stage of etatist regeneration of dogmatic Marxism. On the other hand, in the majority of other societies of the ex-"second" world it is ethnic nationalism that filled the vacuum (luckily, not for long) that formed after the collapse of the official ideology – why not stake on it in Russia, either? Besides, all history, Russia's tradition (from the 13th century?), the alternatives of its development were largely determined by the struggle for the preservation of independence, integrity, the cultural identity of the country, and the overall predominance of the statehood. To a large measure this referred to the times of crisis or the break-up of the historical process. And what is most important, Russia again faces the problems of the new national state identity, national frustration, a menace to lose its independence in international affairs, the full depreciation of its attainments and potential of the national economy. Any strategy or any renewal of the left ideology cannot but take into account these problems; neglecting them, the left are doomed to be a propaganda group or, at best, parliamentary or social opposition.

However, the "national communist" model and the corresponding tactics of this ideology drives the staunch proponents of this tendency out of the margins of the "left space." Elements of militant anti-democratism and refusal of internationalism (de jure or de facto) make this ideology above all fundamentalist, opposing the new trends of the age. This is especially important since we are speaking about advanced industrial society, which is to evolve into post-industrial.

Regardless of whether we speak about the opportunist, "tactical" choice of the least-resistance line and the maximum adaptation or the real change of ideological landmarks, the nationalistic stand of the pseudo-left, combined with the conservative immobilism of the "traditional left" and the proprietary enthusiasm of the former top bureaucracy in economic structures, continued to discredit the ideology and policy of the left as a whole. They represent a force which is unable to offer the project of the future which would be alternative to the policy of the authorities and which could meet the new conditions and necessities. This, combined with the tactics of extremist groups, the weakness and the fragmentation of the renewed democratic left (and left-off the centre groups) and the bipolar vision of the situation, imposed by mass media, naturally led to that the left, perceived by the middle generation, the major part of the intelligentsia and especially the youth, as a sector which belonged to the past by definition and which is ready to start a civil war for the sake of returning to the past.

Society's majority sectors which are disappointed in the right-wing authorities and lost any credit in them do not lean to the left or the "centrists" but are losing any interest in politics in general and in parties, programmes, etc. or support those of them which proclaim what the masses would like to have. In such a situation the left are counteracted by their organization disorder and the ideological pluralism (which in another situation could have become a source of broad influence of the left front) and the lack of authoritative leaders in their ranks. And of course, all the global impulses we have talked about (suffice it to mention such problems, the hardest to the left, as the attitude of the Russian masses towards parties and ideologies and of the youth towards any collective actions). As a result, there is no reason to wonder why the Russian left are so weak even in two to two and a half years when they got rid of the pseudo-left authorities, alien to the people.

Has the situation changed at the turn of 1993 and 1994 and to what extent? What are the short-term and middle term perspectives for the left and left-off-centre trends in Russia and other post-authoritarian societies?

It is generally known and, possibly, accepted that the changes in mass moods acquired a qualitative character: the fire and blood of October 1993 became a catalyst of shifts which ripped in the mass consciousness long ago about the situation in the socio-economic sphere and the problems of law and order. The shelling of the White House in Moscow had a more significant effect on this consciousness than the previous coup d'etat. Today the power (presidential above all) is again regarded by the majority as "they" as power which opposes people, which of course does not preclude the expectations, related with this power.

Following this shift and partly because of it, the relations between the elites (the principal "macrosubject" of Russian society) began to change. From the bipolar confrontation of the elite blocks of the 1992-1993 model these relations tend to attaining consensus; the tendency of the elite consolidation (at the cost of the popular majority) is slowly making its way deep in the political community, and not without contradictions. At the same time another process is developing on the surface of political life: the process of discord within the elite and the struggle for trillions. The corridors of power become as unpredictably dangerous for the careers of political bosses as city streets for the life of new bosses of the economy...

To my mind, the stand of the left and their ability to influence the country's development in the interests of the majority were affected by this shift in society only to a minor extent.

First of all, it was manifest in the election results of the left and left-off-centre groups. As has been noted, contrary to Poland, Lithuania, Hungary and the Ukraine, the real electorate of the Russian left was two to three times smaller than the number of the voters who share the left (socialist and collectivist) values and ideals (according to the public opinion poll – 40 to 50 per cent). The left yielded the greater part of their potential electorate to the Liberal-Democratic Party of Russia and the "party of abstainers", another part to the centrist blocks and groups. To put it another way, the outflow of the masses from the authorities, from the right, from the "anti-communist orientation" in Russia did not get the "left way".

Largely it was determined by the inertia of the specifically national processes we talked about above. And it was not only because of the inertia alone but also because of the mounting progress of some of the processes, especially concerning CPRF's tactics.

What I mean is:

– pedaling the national idea which underlies the programme and the system of unions of parties although, it seems to me, neither the Communist Party of the Russian Federation nor Yeltsin or whosoever will be able to outdo Zhirinovsky;

– the growing tendency (from late November 1993) to ignore and hush up everything that is related with the authoritarian character of the regime and the maxims of the struggle for political democracy in Russia;

– evident involvement of the CPRF leadership in the processes of consolidation of the elite and the clan rivalry to the detriment of the certain socialist stand and clear opposition line.

The successes of the left in Central Europe were based on their social-democratic identity. It may be right to speak in the Ukraine about the social-unionist platform (of international colour). What is suggested in Russia is the state-patriotic idea as a basis of unification and the system of unions of the left. Beyond the "colonial situations" this idea could be neither specifically left nor leading in the left paradigm in the past. The national idea was inseparably united with the democratic (anti-dictatorial) and social ideas in both the situations of anti-Fascist struggle in occupied Europe and in Latin America within the framework of the "revolutionary-anti-imperialist" model. It is the unity of these three lines of struggle that consolidated most effectively its subject – the people – and found a natural complement in international ideology and action. And of course, it is not an ideological expression of a "wave of the future."

It is doubtful whether the "state-patriotic" idea can become an ideological platform for the successful struggle against the savage, capitalist platform, which will surely try to assimilate this ideology. But in any case, it will not be able to become the basis of the political action and influence of the left forces. History demonstrated that in such a union it is the identity of the left, its socialist and democratic component that becomes assimilated. The more so that it will take place in today's Russia.

The current real chances of the left and the left-off-centre forces and the masses they represent are mostly related with a certain phase situation which is common to the "post-authoritarian and neoliberal" countries of the second and third echelon and which is determined by the end of the initial stage of transformation and the reaction of masses to the social results, to the social policy of neoliberal governments.

In the majority f national cases – from Mexico, Honduras, Venezuela (Panama, Uruguay, Costa Rica, etc.) to the Eastern lands of the FRG, Slovakia, Bulgaria, etc. the masses, having paid the costs of reforms (unemployment, the drop and polarization of income, decay of social services, etc.) as well as delays and distortions in their implementation (corruption above all), are striving for changing the course – radically (Brazil, maybe Nicaragua) or partly. The anti-state, anti-collectivist, "individualistic", anti-socialist (Europe) enthusiasm transformation of the previous stage impart to the current motion of the pendulum a character of shift to the left values and orientations (especially in the countries where the right were in office. The situation is more complex if the centrists implemented the "neoliberalization"...). It seems we soon will have quite a few examples of such situations and successes of the left-off-centre (rarely left) forces.

One can single out a number of particular social and socio-psychological moments of this situation, which objectively favour the left forces in Russia.

I mean:

– elements of the active reaction of the masses to the going crisis processes in the economy (especially in industry) and/or in the social sphere. The experience of Lithuania, partly Poland, Brazil and Uruguay testify that a fairly large part of the masses may support the left in such a situation, given certain conditions:

– the position of agricultural sector which, according to the experience of Bulgaria and some other countries of Central Europe (and also Mexico) and the results of voting in 1993, retain the adherence to the former state (collectivist) system, contrary to the dogma but in accordance with the tradition. This tendency may be intensified by the free sale of land.

– almost generally accepted common necessity to return to a greater part of the state in the economic life;

– intensification of the significance and opportunities of the regions and the regional elite to countermand the influence of the centre imbued with the spirit of militant anti-communism;

– the inertia of "values and ideals of socialism" which today outlines the potential influence of the left;

– the fading out of the "one sided anti-communist" orientation of the anti-bureaucratic complex of the mass consciousness, its reorientation against the new ruling groups, their privileges and corruption, the growing "anti-mafia", anti-criminal attitudes of mass consciousness which now work against the neobureaucracy and the financial and commercial elite.

All these are the factors that are now working, and, in this sense, they are undoubtful. Others have a potential character to a certain extent, depending on the course of time and the stand of the left.

They consist in:

– exhausting of the hopes for the temporary transition character of today's shortcomings which should promptly and automatically give way to "normal capitalism" (the effect of purgatory) or bring back the former order of things; realization of the current reality as the natural result of the "1991-1992 choice", the organic and durable state of "post-communist society" (not the "faults of the system but the system of faults");

– the gradual crystallization of the sociophysological and ideological complex of the "struggle of hired labour in the conditions of forming capitalism" (prospective factor);

– the tendency of the anti-authoritarian struggle (to be treated below);

– shifts in the left force proper.

At the same time the additional counterfactors will simultaneously be effective, limiting the influence of the left and neutralizing the opportunities of expansion.

They are:

– the demographic factor: the influence of the left values, ideals and organizations is concentrated among those who are over 50; on the contrary, the youth is the principal vehicle of "non-communism" and to a lesser extent of anti-communism;

– the development of the market relations and adaptation to them, which diminish the "nostalgic complex";

– the growing influence of the private property elite (although this factor seems to be ambivalent in the sense we are interested in);

– the going impact of the "demonstration" and "imitation" effect (in the short term);

– the discrediting of the left by the actions of the "pseudo-left" or by their own passivity, ideological dogmatism or/and political opportunism;

– the persistence of the anti-communist (anti-socialist, anti-collectivist or the like) syndrome among the creative intelligentsia of Russia which undoubtedly has no equals in the modern world, including the USA and Central Europe. On the one hand, this syndrome, broadcast on TV, continues to influence the masses, on the other, diminishes the possibilities of dialogue with the centrists which is so needed for renewal and expansion of the left.

It is hard to say where the dividing line will go between these tendencies. To my mind, this will depend on three principal circumstances: on the character of development of the socioeconomic crisis, the ability of the left to renew and work out an alternative project and on the part played by the left in the struggle against the right-authoritarian tendency, on the outcome of this struggle and further advance along the road of "democracy of participation".

It seems that in the medium-term and long-term perspective this line of struggle will produce the maximum possibilities of ousting "Stalin's gene" for the genuinely left trends and good opportunities to unite their forces and organizations and involve a considerable part of the traditionally left and maybe a part of the present "pseudo-left". Besides, it will promote to convert the movement into a modern left (left-socialist, social-democratic, democommunist, left-democratic, left-humanist, etc.) movement which hinges on a broad mass support (20 to 40 percent of the electorate) in the majority of social and age groups of society, into a movement of "protest and proposal" which is not secluded in an ideological ghetto, a movement which is capable of constructive interaction with the centrist forces and of political coexistence with or opposition to civilized (pluralistic and non-criminal) right trends.

The fact that the goals and "messages" of the left in the Russian situation do not contradict the national-ethnic interests (contrary to, say, the former GDR or Croatia or the Baltic states) and coincide in many respects with the "message" of the post-industrial civilization, drives such a perspective out of the framework of pure Utopia. This is also testified by the current situation in many countries of Central and Southern Europe and Latin America, which develop in the post-authoritarian "space and time". However, there is a strong argument against this: the masses have other business to do than toy with democracy. "It is not 1991". The masses are much more sensitive to the problems of national and social aspects. Almost half the population is ready to sacrifice democratic freedoms and institutions for the sake of curbing corruption, crime and chaos. The word "democracy" compromised itself during the last 36 months no less than socialism over the 75 years. All this is true but, taking into account the situation, we possibly cannot base on it even the medium-term policy, especially in Russia with its tradition. The left forces, which avoid or postpone the struggle for political democracy, are doomed never to attain real progress for society in its struggle for other goals. Neither tomorrow nor the day after tomorrow. Neither the revival of Russia nor social justice is possible at the end of the 20th century when people is deprived of the participation in decision-making. Having formed in the mid-1990s, Russian neoauthoritarianism will creep into the 21st century to settle for long.

One way or another, the realization of the possibility largely, if not entirely, depends on the left proper. The left has possibly no strategic chances beyond the process of "self-transformation", in any case in the long-term perspective or even in the medium-term if one counts on Russia.

But in any case, this process will take time; the time which is needed to recognize and assimilate what is going on, to overcome the dogmatic, nostalgic or self-interested resistance to the very idea of renewal. That is the time required for changing the ideological and political paradigm without refusing from the basic values of the left culture and for working out the new alternative project which is based on real tendencies of development instead of merely stating them; the time for getting back from etatism to the liberating sources of movement and simultaneously for modernizing transformation of its mentality, conventionally from an English and Russian factory of the 19th century, determined by reality, to a new one which would include laboratories and offices of the 21st century, the time for finding the optimum correlation between the traditional and the latest trends of struggle, critical assessment of the road that has been covered and the verity of initial values, traditions and symbols. (All this is a special topic.)

It will take the time, required for overcoming the inertia of the past in the abilities of practical action; the time to imbue the going changes in the consciousness and language, in the relations within and outside of the organization. The time to make all these changes such that they would be received by society as an indispensable block of the new identity of the left rather than a tactical trick.

But time is not neutral. The situation, lost today when new society is crystallizing, may turn tomorrow a narrowing space of political action, reduced to the niche of the propagandist survival...

And lastly, the question from which we should have started. Is there in principle a similar political space for the left in the post-authoritarian and post-industrial world? Are they needed by the social development of the 21st century or are they merely a rudiment of the past, preindustrial and industrial civilization, the situation of the class struggle and the cold war?

This problem has widely been debated since the times of the known article by F. Fukuyama and not without ground (Fukuyama held that the "end of history" was the "end of the left").

Naturally, I am sure that the political space for the left does exist and the left is needed.

They are needed, although in a changed form, for the establishing post-industrial society. Because any shift we have talked about brings about new problems, contradictions and conflicts that are or will be an objective basis for the activity or struggle of the left in civil society.

Since we speak about democracy, this struggle will be for the expansion, democratization of relations within civil society, the relations between the individuals of different sex and age, against the permanent dangers of new bureaucracy and new oligarchies, for the rights of minorities, primarily ethnic, and, above all, for the all-round solution of the problem of participation. The new forms will be acquired by the social struggle, conflicts which cannot be reduced to merely the class struggle (socioeconomic); the struggle for the development (or preservation) of the individual, culture, etc. And each of these spheres will have as the "newest left" the elements, trends and organizations which will come for the most radical solution in the interests of society as a whole, thus changing the result of this solution and overcoming the conservatism of society and especially the ruling and dominating groups in the particular moment.

This especially relates to the basically new lines of struggle which will possibly become, or are already becoming, the principal lines which will determine the mission of the left in the 21st century. What I mean is the solution of global problems, primarily the ecological problem and that of the "North-South" which became most acute in the 1990s.

We should not neglect new, uncertain problems, which may arise in a couple of decades as a result of the current technological cycle ("Kondratyev-52").

Will these movements and left ideologies of the radical vanguard be able to put forth an integral project of the social structure within the "national framework"? It is not clear so far. It seems undoubted that such a project is necessary on the global scale and that it will come to life as a result of variants and alternatives. And it also seems undoubted it will give the "space of the left".

However, we talked so far about the problems which are no more than compulsory landmarks for the future for the majority of humanity part of which is our country, too.

This majority exists in the world the reality of which predicates on the contradictions of the traditional type even though they exercise might pressure from radically new impulses and influences, coming from the centre of the system, on the contradictions and tendencies of development of industrial and pre-industrial societies. And they will remain in such a situation for quite a time: the attempts to "jump over" will hardly be effective for the majority of the countries. What is also possible is variants of partial or full social involution. In these conditions the part that the left can play is more traditional and radical as compared with the post-industrial societies, and their tasks are more simple because many landmarks and attitudes remain as usual and, at the same time, more complex owing to the necessity to combine the past and the future in their activity.

Other things that remain topical include the struggle against the authoritarian tendencies of the old and new oligarchies and authoritarian regimes; the struggle against the crying economic and social inequality, growing in the course of privatization of the economy; the struggle against the diktata and equality in international affairs, against national oppression, ethnic rivalry, genocide and wars.

In other words, the historical mission of the left remains in this world as usual: to represent the interests of the most of the peoples in their confrontation with authoritarianism; working people in their confrontation with the elite; civil society in its confrontation with state centralism; the nation in its conflict with the monopoly of the "centre" in solving the world problems.

But doing all this, the left is called upon to simultaneously orientate themselves towards the maxims of the new, global civilization and change from within.

The left cannot accomplish this mission – the neoliberal alternative will be imposed on society in "pure form", and the resultant tendency of this development, optimum for the majority of society will not be established. Who pays the bill in this case we know from the experience of Latin America, for one.

In other case, the resultant force of this kind will include another vector: the opposition (or the ruling circles) adhering to the non-leftist values will not leave it without any alternative. First of all, this vector may include tendencies of ethnic or religious fundamentalism, national authoritarianism or neoliberal extremism no matter if they are the European ultra-right or the Russian advocates and supporters of Pinochet.

There is no need to explain that everything that has been said has a direct relation to the current situation in Russia and in other countries of the former USSR. Of course, it will be a more complicated business to create an influential and genuinely left (or left-off-centre) coalition here than in other countries. But it seems to me the need in this coalition is maximum, taking into account the specifics of the "initial accumulation of capital" in the country, atomization and social insecurity of the population, the rapid economic slump and sliding down into the "Third World" and the desire of various forces for a "hard guy in office". It is not likely that the force like that may crystallize in Russian, post-authoritarian society and the choice between the Pinochet regime and chaos is quite probable. To put it another way, the question is not in the deficit of the necessity but in the difficulty of its implementation.

"CENTRISM" IN RUSSIAN POLITICS

Oleg Vitte[*]

The predominance of *transition* processes and states in the socio-economic and political reality demands that the researcher should study both the "prospective" phenomena and the specific requirements to the methods of their analysis. Such an approach is extremely important for understanding the processes of systems transformation, which are going on in the territory of the former USSR and the countries of Eastern Europe. However, we must admit one thing: what we expect to be the result of our analysis must practically be obtained as a result of real processes of transformation. Respectively, for a time our analysis results will be variable magnitudes which have been traced at a certain point of the trajectory from their initiation (or an attempt to come to life) to stable forms. This generates serious terminological problems. As a whole, the customary scientific language has been worked out also for the description of stabilized social sciences, at best, for the analysis of the factors, which threaten the stability and, for instance, generate a revolutionary situation. It seems that it is least of all fit for the analysis of the revolutionary epochs proper – the periods of systems transformation. Therefore, in a number of cases we shall specially agree with regard to the terminology used.

One of the first methodological problems of studying transition states consists in classifying in accordance with a *basis unknown in advance*. The analysis of the composition of the State Duma with respect to both the

[*] O. Vitte is a consultant of the government's working centre of economic reforms. The article was first published in Russian in the journal *Polis*, No. 4, 1994.

deputies' political orientations and the group of their interests is no exclusion. The final choice of the classification suggested below was the result of the long preliminary work: we made up a variant of classification according to teach of the multitude of grounds which was then tested with respect to the analysis "productivity" which finally decides the variant's fate.

The author regarded as most productive that type of classification of the deputies' political bias, which accounted for the deputies' division into factions and groups with respect to their readiness to adopt "unpopular" measures in the economy. The latter include first of all the measures of "monetarism" which has almost become a national myth. One margin of the scale which included the most resolutely minded deputies was defined as "right", the other being "left" and the middle the "centre".[1]

According to this division the State Duma can be classified as follows:

the right – YaBloko, Russia's Choice, and the December 12 Union;

the centre – the Democratic Party of Russia (DPR), the Party of the Russian Unity and Accord (PRES), Women of Russia, and the New Regional Policy;

the left – the Agrarian Party, the Community Part of the Russian Federation (CPRF), the Liberal Democratic Party of Russia (LDPR), and the Russian Road.[2]

Although the factions were classified in accordance with the first voting in the State Duma, the further "migration" of the deputies did not alter the general alignment of forces in principle.

It was much harder to find a more significant classification of the deputies according to the groups of interest or, to put it more accurately, according to

---

[1] The use of the terms "left" and "right" should not lead the reader astray. The current tradition regards the communists as the left and the adherents of the liberal market as the right. This is the only ground to define the political blocs with these terms instead of using Nos. 1 and 2. The same refers to the notion "centre". The "centrists" are defined by the only criterion – uncertainty of the position according to the basic differentiating feature. We will speak about the specifics of the Russian "centrism" below.

[2] Regardless of the specific interest to the party programmes of the LDPR, having neo-imperial intentions, and the Russian Road group, the decisive significance in Russia's nearest history will belong to the economic policy. The cited associations have more in common with the communists.

the character of their ties with the economic interest.[3] The outcome of this effort
is as follows:

1. The representatives of the economic organizations (these include
enterprises of all forms of property and the line of business which earn profit).

2. The representatives of the state body (federal, regional and local) which
are related with the economy, i.e. the state economic departments *–the*
"economic officials".

3. The representatives of the state bodies which are not related with the
economy of all levels – *"non-economic officials"*.

The analysis shows that the discrepancies between the interests of the two
latter groups are so great that their corporative community becomes merely an
auxiliary circumstance.[4] On the contrary, the political orientation of the
economic officials is fairly close to the representatives of the economic
organizations, which allows in a number of cases to consider them together in
the same group.

4. Deputies who are not related either with economic activity or with the
state bodies – "pure politicians" or *"ideologists"*.

One may suppose that the deputies of the first two groups are more inclined
to defend the interests of their industries than the deputies of the last two
groups, in any case, the connection with these interests is quite manifest and
stable. However, the "non-economic officials" and "ideologists" may be
attracted to lobbying for the sake of their industries (especially in regions)
directly or indirectly by defending the regional interests, which is more
probable.

---

[3] No stable groups of interest have formed in Russia so far and will not form for a certain time.
In such conditions one of the most general and significant grounds for differentiation according
to interests will be the difference by the degree, strength and direction of the effect of
economic processes as a major source of forming the future interests. It is evident that a
director of an enterprise and, say, a journalist will experience a different impact of the
interest-framing factors. Possibly it would be more exact to name the cited groups the "groups
of the closeness to the interests." However, for the sake of shortness they will be called the
group of interests.

[4] I mean exactly the Duma deputies. It is much more difficult to identify the differences
between the two groups of the officials in the actions of the local elite in preparing for and
conducting the election (in one-mandate districts).

The analysis that has been carried out allows getting answers to several groups of questions: (a) does the alignment of political forces in the Duma deviate from the real alignment of forces in society? (b) which side is it slanting? (c) to what extent? (d) which factors motivate this deviation? The analysis of data was carried out along three lines: the representation of industries' interests in the Duma and their real weight in society, the correlation of the political blocs in the Duma as a whole and among the deputies from the regions, and the correlation of the political blocs in the Duma as a whole and among the deputies, elected in one -mandate districts.

It should be noted that the survey has not revealed any strong dependence on various factors. *All generalized data and conclusions, suggested below, were made exclusively on the analysis of weak dependencies and finding their real value via the correlation with a broader socio-political context.*

The correlation of forces in the Duma does not give any absolute advantage to any of the three political blocs and does not allow any of them to dominate.

Political blocs in the Duma:

the right	29%
the centrists	30%
the left	41%

According to the adherence to group interests the deputies fall into three parts, close in their number, if the first two groups of interests are combined into one of those having direct economic interests.

The groups of interests in the Duma:

representatives of economic organizations	23%
"economic officials"	14%
two first groups together	37%
"non-economic officials"	24%
"ideologists"	37%

The character of the distribution of the representatives of the groups of interests according to the political blocs allows identifying the most important elements of the social base of the latter from the point of view of their ability to influence the political process.

The left are most influential among the representatives of economic organizations and the "economic officials" (half of the deputies of this type are left) on the one hand, and "ideologists" (more than half) on the other. One can identify here a strongly manifest division of labour: the major bulk of "ideologists" belongs to the LDPR faction[5] , and a little less to the CPRF while the Agrarian Party is not represented although it command strong positions in the groups, representing the economic organizations and the "economic officials".

The centrists rank second among the representatives of economic organizations and the "economic officials" (about a third of the deputies of these groups) as well as among the "non-economic officials" (42 per cent).

The right are most influential among the "non-economic officials" (half of the deputies of this group) and the "ideologists" (more than a quarter). Only those of the "economic officials" tend right who represent the departments, connected with the on-going privatization.

What is interesting, however, is the fact that the left predominance in the Duma is maintained by a high rate of representation of the only industry – the *Agroindustrial complex* (actually the whole of the Agrarian Party). Counting out the deputies, related with the Agroindustrial complex, the left in the first group (the representatives of economic organizations) ranks second and even third in the second group (the "economic officials"). In this case the centrists unambiguously rank first in both groups.

Furthermore, the influence of the left in the first group (excluding the AIC) belongs to the deputies who are *not leaders of enterprises* (in the majority of cases they are workers and petty officers from the Communist faction).[6] If one takes into account only the deputies who are leaders, the centrist predominance

---

[5] The LDPR faction differs from the three others (the Agrarian Party, the Russia's Choice and the Communists) by one specific feature: its influence on the officialdom (both in Moscow and in regions) comes to zero)

[6] The fact that we leave aside the classic contradiction between the employer and the employee is connected with that in today's Russia the contradictions between the state and the commercial sectors are manifested more vividly than the contradiction between the labour and capital.

becomes even more impressive while the representation of the left diminishes practically to the level of the right.

Thus, if one excludes *the AIC deputies and those who are not managers from the groups of interests which exert the greatest influence on the economic policy, even the absolute predominance of the left among the "ideologists" who are manned more than by half by the LDPR will not be enough to make the majority or even rank the second.* The predominance of the "non-economic officials" (given the said amendments) allows the right to occupy that place.

The unexpected political liking of the "non-economic officials" needs to be explained. I can suggest the following hypothesis. The legal privatization of the state property that was going since deep processes of the disintegration of the so-called administrative command system prepared 1992 that began in the 1960s. During this period that can be called a period of "initial privatization" a broad social layer of people formed who really pretended to disintegrate the state property and legalize the results of the fact. The discrepancies of interests of the economic and non-economic officials are evident: what the former can obtain in the usual way in the working conditions without any "politics" can be obtained by the latter only given the strong organized political support.

In order to assess the prospects of the *direct lobbying of industries and the potential political claims of the representatives of various industries*, one should consider the composition of the first two groups of interests in greater detail. The following classification appeared to be quite promising.

1. *The representatives of economic enterprises.*

Enterprises of the AIC.

Industrial enterprises of other industries.

    1) Heavy processing industry, the military-industrial complex (MIC).

    2) Raw materials industries.

    3) Light and food industries, construction.

Trade and financial enterprises.

2. *Economic officials.*

Agroindustrial complex.

Industries.

Leadership of the privatization.

General leadership of the economy.[7]

The significance of the Agroindustrial complex has been established above: *it is only the left political bloc (to be more exact the Agrarian Party alone) that has distinct industrial interests and it is the AIC that formed, without any support, a strong parliamentary faction to defend its own interests.*

The political orientation of other industries and services hardly manifests itself. Thus, the political sympathies of the deputies who are professionally related with trade and financial enterprises or companies (they exceed the amount of the AIC representatives) are practically scattered over all blocs. This may probably be explained by the fact that these branches of economic activity are most successful in the present conditions and, therefore, the subjective political bias of the deputies who represent them is not so rigidly motivated by the objective economic interests. Today the latter are differentiated mainly depending on the acuteness of the crisis in their industry and the ways of surviving. The results of the "natural selection" may be fixed, following a certain time (beyond the bounds of the short-term interests): the most promising methods of *surviving* may keep on as the new forms of *normal life.*

The heavy processing and raw materials industries have half the amount of the usual representation, the light and food industries have still less than that. The MIC proper is hardly represented at all.

Orientations of the Duma deputies from the heavy processing industry manifest themselves in two different forms. As has been said, the blue and white collars sympathize unambiguously with the left. Naturally, the leadership of their "own enterprises" has certain expectation, related with the activity of their "own" deputies. However, the political orientations of the leaders proper who are the Duma deputies are evenly disseminated over all political blocs.

One may suppose that the current situation in Russia is dominated by *political independence and organization of a certain level, representing industries' interests, proportionate to the state of archaic economic orders, which are capable of effecting the tolerable existence of the particular industry.* Economic forms permanently change without having time to acquire

---

[7] The two last subgroups are not taken into account.

the stability, which is necessary to be politically formulated. Only those forms may seem to be stable which are remnants of the former political system as well as the illusions, which help believe that these forms will not further disintegrate.

The general situation is somewhat distorted by the deputies who are related with the raw materials industry. Although they do not have independence from the Duma factions to defend their own interests and are hardly capable of following suit of the Agrarian Party, their political bias is quite evident, tending towards the "centrist" political bloc. Possibly, another specific factor of politicized interests is effective in this case.

Given the current structural crisis, only raw materials producers manage to remain competitive on the would market, and not all of them. However, what regards the domestic "bureaucratic market" of resources redistribution, the processing industry, too, succeed to remain competitive. Such "social injustice" explains the politicized attitude of the raw materials producers.

The analysis of the direct representation of industries allows making the following conclusion. The industries will defend their interests mostly not in the Duma but using the regional deputations, which are united, by an aggregate interest of a group of producers of the particular territory rather than the interests of the particular industries. Respectively, mighty factors will be effective, splitting the unity of industries' interests, on the one hand, and bringing closer the interests of local inter-branch complexes on the other. In other words, *it is not probable that a significant, organized lobby of industries might form in the Duma to oppose the government.* The Agroindustrial complex will be an exception.

The comparison of data on the Duma as a whole and its regional part (i.e. without the deputies from Moscow) shows that the nominal composition of the Duma distorts the real alignment of forces in society.

Political blocs among the deputies from regions[8] :

the right	24%	(29%)
the centrists	35%	(30%)
the left	40%	(41%)

---

[8] Hereinafter we given in brackets the data referring to the whole of the Duma.

On the whole, the correlation of the political blocs among the regional deputies repeats that in the Duma, however, the share of the centrists is markedly higher because of the reduced share of the right and the left to some extent.

We have similar shifts in the first two groups of interests. The left has somewhat greater influence in the group of the "non-economic officials" from regions, remaining third in significance. The centrists go to the forefront in this case, ousting the right who rank second. Finally, the "ideologists", too, keep up the usual correlation of forces in the Duma. However, in this case, too, the centrists somewhat increase their influence, remaining third in significance.

Thus, *the centrists in regions are the main reformatory blocs, replacing the right as the principal competitor of the left in the basic group of the right – the "non-economic officials", increasing their share in all other groups.*

If one takes into account that the excessively politicized attitudes of the Moscow dwellers distort the real picture of interests of the basic groups of the population, the regional representation appears to be more exact than that of the Duma as a whole in manifesting the balance of interests in society and the corresponding alignment of political forces, one should admit *the composition of the Duma does not tally with the real picture of the political sympathies in Russian society, markedly diminishing the influence of the centrists.*

The election of half of the deputies on the party lists significantly altered the alignment of forces in the Duma as compared with the possible results if the election were based on the majority system. The correlation of the political blocs in the Duma among the deputies, elected in one-mandate districts and the whole body of deputies illustrates this fact:

the right	34%	(29%)
the centrists	36%	(30%)
the left	30%	(41%)

On the whole, *the party lists appeared to be more beneficial for the left* (being last, they came to the forefront) and *most detrimental to the centrists* (being first, they now rank second). On the average in all groups of interests, the centrists lost the relative majority, yielding to the left.

If we consider the first two groups of interests who are directly related with the economy, the relatively great losses of the centrists compared with the losses of the right are even more impressive. The right remained in the same third place. While the centrists lost the first place (they shared it with the left) the left gained practically the absolute majority (half of the deputies are in these groups).

The shift to the left is not so manifest in the regions although its direction is the same.

The correlation of forces in the political blocs in the regional part of the Duma among the deputies, elected in the one-mandate districts, and the deputies as a whole is as follows:

the right	27%	(24%)
the centrists	41%	(35%)
the left	33%	(40%)

In all groups of "interests" the regional centrists lost the relative majority, yielding it to the left, and in the first two groups (and in the Duma as a whole) the actual majority which they shared with the left. The share of the right in these groups diminished insignificantly.

The right suffered the most detrimental defeat from the left *only in Moscow*. However, one should take into account the fact that the Moscow deputation grew at the cost of the party lists almost six times (from 27 to 154 deputies) while the regional one grew by a mere 43 per cent (from 200 to 286).

What is typical is that the Moscow majority of the right in the one-mandate districts was sufficient to maintain the second place in the Duma as a whole, yielding it to the left among the deputies, elected from the regions.

* * * * * *

In order to incorporate the analysis results into a broader socio-political context, we will have to consider two issues in greater detail: what is centrism in Russia and what are the motives of the differing results of the election by the party lists and the one-mandate districts?

As experience shows the practice of state centrism, i.e. one that is effective in the system of state power (contrary to the purely ideological centrism of the party groupings) consists in conducting a moderately rigid or "quasi-monetary" financial policy under "anti-monetary" but reformatory-market slogans. In other words, the real Russian centrism (on economic grounds) is a moderately right policy under moderately left slogans.

This means that the Russian centrism is devoid of ideology of its own and for that reason contrary to the right and left, is hardly capable of forming electrical political organizations of its own. Hence the failures of all attempts of the centrist party building.

The space of the centrist policy is not maintained by its own organizations but purely by the desire of the right and left organizations to impose unilaterally its political will to society in combination with the impossibility of implementing such desires.

It is evident furthermore that the results of the elections by the party lists less dependence on the local elite than the results of the elections in one-mandate districts. Therefore, the former were more accurate in expressing the moods of Russia's population (the man in the street) than the latter. But one should bear in mind that the "ideals" and "interests" play a different part in the orientations of the elite and the rest of the population.

Without going into detail with respect to the problems of ideals and interests, let us dwell only on those aspects of this opposition, which are important for discussing the results of our analysis. It would hardly be right to regard that, contrary to interests, ideals as motives are free from the influence of people's real social status. Undoubtedly, the ideals (if we take into account the majority of people only) are the most stable part of the motives, and the real change of them requires stronger and more durable influence. In other words, the shifts in the social status are more likely to change interests than the ideals. The more so, ideals often remain the only trace of the vanishing social states whose reflection had been erased in the interests.

At the same time, ideals may undergo superfluous changes, which make believe that the past has been done over with. It is exactly this kind of changes that include the change of socialist and communist ideals for anti-communist and the other way around. Not once have the numerous polls proven an evident thing: anti-communism is a mere desire to get what the communists promised by driving them out of office for failing to accomplish their commitments. In general, the ideal motivations can be changed according to the following algorithm: deep, essential shifts begin when all possible attempts to avoid superfluous changes are exhausted.

New interests of various strata of Russian society form as a result of privatization (in the broad sense) of the state property. But since realty (primarily land) is least of all involved in this process, the fragments of the ruling elite, filling in the institutes of state power, turn into the centres of gravity for all forming groups of interests. Actually, these fragments of the ruling elite appear to be the most organized (and the only) carriers of what deserves to be called interests. The political behavior of the rest of society is determined predominantly by values and ideals. Even such organizations as association of businessmen or directors of state enterprises (if they are really independent) are quite uncertain in the field of interests.

I would not simplify the matter if I say that the voting in one-mandate districts showed real interests of Russian society while the voting by the party lists showed its ideals. The above discrepancies in the results of this voting were the outcome of the divergence between the interests and the ideals.

Taking into account all that has been said, we can identify the following facts.

The political orientations, connected with real economic interests, unambiguously tend towards the centrist political bloc while the orientations free from any interest towards the left. In that case the influence of the right on those who orientate on their ideals and interests practically coincides, yielding to the other two blocks.

If we sum up the existing orientations to ideals and interests, we can say that society put forth an order to the state to *retain the centrism that has established over the two years, moving it a little leftwards in what regards the slogans.*[9] In other words, by performing such a policy, the government may count on the maximum socio-political stability of society.

---

[9] Such a social order is a Russian "reflection" of social moods in all countries which

The alignment of the political forces in the Duma that set up diminishes the influence of the centrists in society almost exclusively at the cost of the exaggerated representation of the left. This shift of the political scale leftwards is mainly motivated by two circumstances: the election of 50 per cent of the deputies by the party lists and the high representation of the AIC interests without any reasonable proportion. *The evident interest of the centrists may be accomplished in one way only: by way of the parliamentary union with the right.*

The analysis of the deputy body composition allows understanding the reasons for the election's "unexpected" results. The relative failure of the right or, to be more exact, the false expectations of their great success, is mainly motivated by misunderstanding the shifts that took place during the last three to four years in the sphere of ideals and interests as well as the essence of these shifts in the conditions when one half of the deputies should be elected according to their ideals and the other according to their interests. Without counting on a wider social base that would vote according to interests, the right analysts hoped that the social base would remain at the level of the late 1980s and the voters would vote according to the ideals (i.e. anti-communism). They miscalculated: it so happened that the left had lost their influence in the field of interests (yielding it to the centrists) and regained it in the field of ideals (ousting the right from there).

The social order as defined determines the space for maneuver of he political forces that try to consolidate their influence in society, meaning not only ideals but interests as well.

---

experience similar economic and political transformations: for instance, in Poland and Lithuania (possibly the Ukraine, too) where new governments continued, using moderately left slogans, the moderately right policy, initiated by their predecessors under the opposite slogans.

SPONTANEITY AND CIVILIZATION: TWO FACTORS IN RUSSIA'S FATE

Vladimir Kantor[*]

Today's disorder, spontaneity in all fields of Russia's life, instability of social structures the reformers could rely on urges us to reassess the way Russia has gone moving towards the totalitarian Bolshevik state and, as a result, find a way out of the present crisis.

Back in the past century Chaadaev, when analyzing the historical tendencies of Russia's development, came to realize the permanent feature in Russia's life in the "impersonal chaos", the absence of guarantees of property rights and the individual freedom, and the total suppression of the individual. The result of this was permanent readiness of Russian people to metaphysical and actual riot against any legal norms. In that sense the Russian people has always been equal to the Russian government. In the Russian mentality liberty is opposed to the notion of freedom, having a restriction of freedom of another individual. This diagnosis was proved in the works by Dostoyevsky who showed that the devastating riot might come out of "Karamazov's spontaneity". "There is no ground for our society, it hasn't lived up to rules because it hasn't had any life, either. A colossal upheaval and everything breaks up, tumbles

[*] V. Kantor, D. Sc. (Philos.), an expert in the history of Russian culture, author of the book *In Search for the Personality the Experience of the Russian Classics*. The article was first published in Russian in the journal *Voprosy filosofii*, No. 1, 1994.

down as if it had not existed. And it is not only from the outside like in the West, but internally, morally"[1], wrote Dostoyevsky.

Unfortunately, the Russian revolutionary democrats were deaf and dumb to these precautions. After the revolutionary riot of 1905 the known collection *Vekhi* (Landmarks) reiterated the precautions of Russian thinkers about the danger of revolutionary call in the country which had not formed the norms of civil society, that attempts at the revolutionary restructuring of such a country might turn it into the state of primordial chaos and the destruction of those European features that formed by the end of the 19th century. But the thinkers' precautions have never had historical influence. In 1918 after the total collapse of all norms and forms of civilized life and when it was not clear whether the Bolsheviks would win N. Berdyaev formulated the state of Russian mentality in the following way: "The human personality drowns in our country in the primitive collectivism... It is utterly insignificant whether this all-devouring collectivism will be that of the Black Hundred or the Bolsheviks. The Russian land lives under the power of pagan spontaneity. Any individual drowns in this spontaneity for it is incompatible with personal dignity and personal responsibility..."[2]

Strictly speaking, Stalinism turned to be an ossified form of this spontaneity in which arbitrariness typical of it was extolled to the rank of state policy. All guarantees of the property rights, the individual's honour and dignity, which prop the European civilization, were destroyed. After the collapse of the Communist dictatorship and the disintegration of the empire when the former power structures which rested on the lawlessness in the form of the law were eliminated we seemed to have only one thing left which was lawlessness complemented with the Russian spontaneity which was not restrained even by the state arbitrariness and which opposed the norms of civilized life. One can understand this situation and determine a possible trend of development only in the context of Russian history. It is no accident that the present situation is so often compared with various periods of our history. Here

---

[1] F.M. Dostoyevsky, *Complete Works*, in 30 vols. Leningrad, 1976, Vol. 16, p. 329 (in Russian).

[2] N. Berdyaev, "Ideas and Life", *Russkaya mysl*, Moscow-Petrograd, 1918, Nos. 1-2, p. 105

is for instance the point of view of historian Yu. Afanasyev published by the *Izvestia* newspaper: "In fact, we still remain a traditional Moscow kingdom. When the power slackens everything begins to disintegrate and get into turmoil."[3] The accuracy of this comparison may be disputed but the remnant social, political and spiritual structures of Kiev, Tartar, Moscow, Peter's and Stalin's Russia today became undoubtedly activated as it usually is the case in periods of radical shifts.

A major issue which influences the fat of both Russia and the whole civilization consists in that whether Russia's present society finds a civilized method of taming the chaos or it again slides to the trail of war and dictatorship. In that case the catastrophe may turn to be even more devastating than the outcome of the Bolshevik revolution. One should not forget that Russia possesses nuclear weapons and nuclear power stations, which may destroy the whole world if the civil war is waged. It is for that reason we need to thoroughly analyze these two parameters (the spontaneity and civilization) of Russia's development, their correlation and the lines of opposition if we want to understand the processes going on in Russia.

I. Spontaneity and Civilization as a Problem of Russian History

Recently before the collapse of the USSR when the Communists were afraid of the people's revolt they were prepared to support sober voices warning of the danger of the infuriated crowd which today they, together with the nationalists, try to wake up, counting that the strike will be delivered against their opponents.

Ivan Bunin in his book *Cursed Days* gave the most illustrative definition of the revolution and the civil war in Russia: "A revolution is one of the elements... An earthquake, an epidemic of plague or cholera is also the

---

(in Russian).

[3] Yu. Afanasyev, "The Defeat at the Congress Does not Deprive Us of Optimism", *Izvestia*, March 19, 1993, p. 5.

elements. However, nobody extols or canonizes them – they are to be fought with and controlled."[4]

When does it become possible to fight with plague and cholera? Possibly, when the humanity attains a certain level of civilization and becomes capable of producing remedies and vaccines.

A) A PROBLEM FORMULATION

While reasoning about the specifics of Russian mentality, Chaadaev believed that it manifests itself in the dominance of irregular elements, in chaos and disorganized social and spiritual life. Such is the part played by Russia in the alignment of world forces. According to the Russian philosopher the harmonizing aspect which appeared to be balanced and ordered, despite the past cataclysms and turmoil, consists in the geocultural formation which is outer with respect to Russia – Western Europe which worked out over the long years of civilization the norms of existence: "the ideas of duty, justice, law, order... Such is the atmosphere of the West; this is something more than history and psychology, this is a physiology of the European".[5] Since Chaadaev's times, such a comparison has become permanent in Russian thought. There were times when, contrary to the European "philistine order", people were proud of this Russian spontaneity, sometimes they feared it, hoping for the wholesome effect of the European rules and principles.

What are the elements, spontaneity? It is evident that the matter is not in the vocabulary meaning but in its historical definition, which this entity acquired in the writings of the Russian thinkers. In Russian historiography the notion of the "elements" goes side by side with such notions as "chaos", "barbarism", "savagery," "nature" in its devastating function (volcanoes, earthquakes) and opposes such notions as "cosmos", "culture", "civilization", "logos", "enlightenment", etc. For instance, Berdyaev was sure that there was a dark element in the Russian land and Russian people: "This dark Russian element is reactionary in the deepest sense of the word. It contains an eternal,

---

[4] I. Bunin, *The Cursed Days*, Moscow, 1918, p. 52 (in Russian).
[5] P. Ya. Chaadaev, *Works*, Moscow, 1989, p. 20 (in Russian)

mystic reaction against any culture, against the individual, his rights and dignity, against all kind of values"[6]. In this context civilization is the highest form, the highest stage of culture. Russian thought did not know any other opposition until the book of Spengler, which imparted a negative colouring to the notion of civilization. Without referring even to the thinkers of the liberal-democratic progressive trend, I will only remind the reasoning of N. Danilevsky who believed that the period of civilization was the period of emergence and development of poetry, art, science, philosophy, statehood and other phenomena which extol human society and protect it from the whims of nature.[7]

The European tradition retains even in the 20th century the conception that the civilization period has had a wholesome part in the history of humanity (possibly, without the Russian experience).

Speaking about the importance of culture in the nature, Freud remarked that the nature elements were not yet tamed at all, that the earth sort of ridiculed the human effort to tame it, sending hurricane, typhoons, floods, volcano eruptions and earthquakes to level down the human effort. The Russian thinkers might add to this the invasion of barbarians, which they always regarded as a natural calamity. I would remind Herzen's prophecy about another destruction of the West-European civilization (after the fall of Ancient Rome): "Can't you see new Christians, setting to build; new barbarians, setting to destroy? They are ready; like lava they are moving under the ground, within the mountains. The time will come and Herculaneum and Pompeii will disappear, the good and the evil, and the right and the wrong will perish nearby. It will be neither the court of justice nor reprisal, it will be a cataclysm, a revolution...".[8] In other words, the implementation of the ideals of socialism which Herzen first related with the European proletariat and later only with Russia and the Russian community was equal to him to a geological cataclysm, the nature elements that would annihilate all attainments of the civilization. These ideas and images were brought about by the Russian reality.

---

[6] N. Berdyaev, *The Fate of Russia*, Moscow, 1918, p. 52 (in Russian).
[7] N. Ya. Danilevsky, *Russia and Europe*, St. Petersburg, 1889, p. 111 (in Russian).
[8] A.I. Herzen, *Collected Works*, in 30 vols., Moscow, 1955, Vol. VI, p. 58 (in Russian).

However, a question arises: can the spontaneous humankind (not counting the invasion of barbarians) destroy one's own civilization, which was built by generations? To make the answer more accurate I want to remind that traditionally the scientific writings mark several stages in the formation of culture: savagery, barbarism and civilization which distinguish from each other in the degree of the culture of nature. Various historical types of society are more or less successful. In those cases when civilization did not become quite organic for the culture or, say, was not rooted in it the danger remains that it may get back to barbarism. The revival is also possible in highly developed countries – "inner barbarism does not essentially differ in consequences from an invasion of "barbarians from outside". Ortega and Gasset who saw a "revolt of the masses" in Bolshevism and Fascism, a sort of "vertical invasion of the barbarians" and "significant regress"⁹ protested against the apology for spontaneous instincts which allegedly were inherent in creative development and asserted that the degree of culture was measured by the degree of development of norms.¹⁰ Further on he wrote: "Civilization is not 'just there', it is not self-supporting. It is artificial and requires the artists or the artisan."¹¹ It is civilization that is in need of creative activity.

Unfortunately, the most influential proponents of Russian spirituality, warning about the pending calamities and cataclysms, failed to find an antidote against the spontaneous forces of their culture. The more so, even Dostoyevsky was, from Freud's point of view, inapt as a social healer or moralist. Freud wrote that as a moralist he reminded the barbarians of the epoch of the peoples' migration, the barbarians who killed and then repented of what they had done – in that case the repentance became a technical trick, which cleared the way to new killings. Ivan the Terrible did the same thing; such a deal with one's consciousness was a typical Russian trait.¹² In the long run, the October developments were brought about not only by the "revolutionary devils" but also by other trends of Russian thought that tried to find in the masses' spontaneity the positive basis for building a "new world" (from the ideas of

---

⁹ Jose Ortega y Gasset, *The Revolt of the Masses*, New York, 1932, p. 95.

¹⁰ Ibid., p. 79.

¹¹ Ibid., p. 97.

community and Orthodox God-chosen religion in the Slavophiles and
Dostoyevsky to the apology for plunder and the communal integrity in Bakunin
and Nechaev). As a result, the power of people's spirit was reversed to
destruction of everything that was alien to the popular masses rather than to
creation, which excludes going into raptures and suggests self-criticism,
discipline and enthusiasm instead of the traditional compulsory labour.

According to Russian philosopher B. Vysheslavtsev, the sensation of chaos
as a basis of world order is typical of the October revolution, which in fact
destroyed all civilized structures that had formed by that time in the country. It
should be mentioned that back in the past century Russian scientists came to
believe that civilization promoted preservation of humankind by developing and
protecting the individual[13] and, therefore, the impact of spontaneous forces
should be regarded as a calamity. That is why, according to Vysheslavtsev,
"the spontaneous nature is felt by every Russian as an essence of Russian soul,
Russian character, Russian fate and even Russian nature that cannot be
recognized or translated..."[14]

B) SLAVONIC MYTHOLOGY AND ORTHODOX CHRISTIANITY

Possibly the feeling of spontaneity as the essence of Russian soul is related
with the initial moment when our mentality began to develop, with the fact that
Slavonic mythology was not properly elaborated (vague definition of the
pantheon of all gods) and did not know cosmognonic myths with their major
topic: the transformation of chaos into cosmos: Fyodor Buslaev, the great
Russian philologist of the past century, wrote that "Slavonic mythology did not
follow the pace set by the mythologies of Greece, Scandinavian countries or
Finland in creating all-round, complete types of gods and till now keeps living
with the sincere faith in a number of mythic creatures, although minor,
insignificant ones."[15]

---

[12] S. Freud, *Gesammelte Werke*, Vol. 12, 1947, Berlin, p. 245.
[13] I.I. Mechnikov, *The Sketches of Optimism*, Moscow, 1988, p. 186 (in Russian).
[14] B.P. Vysheslavtsev, *Dostoyevsky and the Spontaneity*, Berlin, 1923, p. 5.
[15] F. Buslaev, *About Literature*, Moscow, 1990, p. 35 (in Russian).

The Slavonic paganism does not know of a "cultural hero", either, i.e. a hero who liberates, civilizes and transforms the land. Such heroes appear in Russia only on the basis of Christianity in the 11th-12th centuries. When Russian writers and thinkers of the 19th century wrote about the danger of revival of the Russian paganism (embodied by Dostoyevsky in Karamazov's violent spontaneity), they saw in that not only rejection of Christianity but a literal return to lower mythology which rejects "the individual in the very essence of it by its own sensuous nature"[16] that did not know of the opposition between the Light and the Darkness, the Good and the Evil and, therefore, remained historically fruitless, devoid of the stimulus to historical progress.

Orthodox Christianity played in Russia a part of the myth-creating structure, introducing into the consciousness of Russian people the principal notions of good and evil, the creation of the universe, and overcoming chaos. As is known, Russia adopted Christianity from Byzantium. Since then, people often argued about the use of such a choice, explaining the drawbacks of the Russian development by the confessional form of Christianity – Orthodoxy with its papism, the dependence of Church and its subordination to the secular authority of emperors. I should add that at that very moment, i.e. the 10th century, the Byzantine Christianity, polished in the philosophic school of antiquity, was both theologically and philosophically more elaborate and more sophisticated than the Roman. As one of the major experts in mediaeval Europe holds "for Byzantines and Moslems the integration into the Roman Christian world would have signified a decay and transition to a lower stage of civilization".[17] Therefore, the choice of the confession was well grounded for Kievan Rus. In the two centuries that followed since the Baptism Kievan Rus had gone through the social, cultural and spiritual uprise. Books were translated, foreign (primarily Greek and Latin) languages studied, towns built and temples erected; the trade with the whole world and especially with Europe and Byzantium was activated and the code of laws – *Russkaya pravda (Russian Truth)* – was written...

---

[16] V.S. Solovyov, *Collected Words*, in 10 vols., St. Petersburg, Vol. 1, p. 22.
[17] Jacques Le Goff. *La Civilisation de l'occident medieval,* Paris, 1977, p. 176.

Naturally, there are various degrees of assimilating Christian conceptions – from the highest theology of the monks to a blend of paganism and Christianity of the commonalty. Common people's spiritual verses give a true conception of the average level of the religious development of a people. However, according to G. Fedotov, a most thorough analyst of the Russian spiritual life, " the study of the religious contents of spiritual verses leads us to the supreme layers of the people's masses that are closely related with the Church world rather than to the dark medium of paganism"[18] Of course, the influence of these layers may appear decisive in the course of time. But the ideas of Christianity were not properly assimilated in people's minds owing to the tragic historical development of Russia and the dual role of the Church. After Russia had been conquered by the Tartars, the Orthodox Church had to fawn to the conquerors, praying for the Khan, and thus the Church became related with the state interests more than it was in Byzantium. Nevertheless, encouraging the rivalry of the princes, the invaders supported Orthodoxy, feeling its importance. Only Church could provide for the spiritual obedience of all Russia regardless of the locality where people lived. Nevertheless, we should note the ambivalence of the situation: in this way the Orthodox Church facilitated Russians to retain the image of the single people although the clergy performed the fiscal, spiritual and police functions. By the moment that Moscow, not without the support of the Khan authorities, began to conquer the rest of Russia and later, using the disintegration of the Golden Horde to its own avail, get rid of the Horde's influence, the Orthodox Church made a stake on the new force and began to actively help Moscow in "collecting" Russian lands. As a result, the habit to play the fiscal part, observing rituals only formally, led to that the Church failed to influence the souls of its parish, merely civilizing them. Already in the 18th century during Catherine the Great's rule G. Orlov, a nobleman, wrote to Jean-Jacques Rousseau that Russian priests could neither dispute nor pray and the parish could only cross themselves, believing that was enough to be Christians. Actually, the popular movement for Christianity began in the second half of the 17th century after the split. But even in the 20th century

---

[18] G. Fedotov, *Spiritual Verses. The Russian Popular Belief in Spiritual Verses*, Moscow, 1991, p. 15 (in Russian).

Goergy Fedotov stated: "We still retain the natural, pre-Christian fundamentals of the popular soul better than all other peoples of culture."[19]

Orthodoxy has never (till the "neo-Orthodox renaissance" of the early 20th century) been related with any social movement which intended to improve people's life or promote the spiritual and social progress and therefore turned to be alien to the real social interests of people. Suffice it to cite even the proponents of Orthodoxy who realize that the immobility of Russian life hinges on the stubborn conservatism of Russian Orthodoxy which is "suspicious to any social and cultural progress".[20] It is no accident that many representatives of the nobility of the past century who were seeking a social transforming force in Christianity reversed to Catholicism (M. Lunin, P. Chaadaev, V. Pecherin et al.). By 1905 a situation set up which marked a growing economic, political, social, religious and cultural crisis which demanded a radical and prompt action. But Orthodoxy could not assist in solving the problem: the great socially creative power of Christianity was not utilized – the Russian Church was devoid of its own independent social stand which did not promote free spiritual development.

This is how S. Bulgakov assessed the situation: "The great people which is helpless and *spiritually defenceless* (italics are mine - V.K.) like a baby that is at the level of enlightenment of St. Vladimir times, and the intelligentsia which carries the Western enlightenment, using mostly the last words which promptly alternate one another like fashion and which, in the long run, will surely find the way to the baby no matter how one tries to hold it. The two types of electricity: when they join one another what will they produce – the beneficial light and heat or the incinerating lightning?"[21] As we now know the Russian life was struck by an incinerating lightning, burning out the elements of the European and Christian civilization in its Orthodox variant which had been worked out over the long hard years of historical development. In 1918 S. Bulgakov summed up the situation, using the words of a character of his from "At the

---

[19] G. Fedotov, *The New Burg. A Collection of Articles, New York, 1952, p. 81.*

[20] A. Elchaninov, P. Florensky. "Orthodoxy", *History of Religion,* Moscow, 1909, p. 183 (in Russian).

[21] S. Bulgakov, "On the Contradictory Nature of the Modern Non-Religious World Outlook (the Intelligentsia and the Revolution)", op. cit., p. 243.

Gods' Feast" (which was later introduced into the collection *From the Depth*), in the following way: "Although we had little ground to believe in the God-bearing people, it was nevertheless expected that the Church that existed a thousand years would be able to tie itself with the people's soul to become precious and desirable. But it happened that the Church was neutralized without any struggle as if it were not needed by people and this was done easier in the country than in town... Suddenly the Russian people turned to be non-Christian..."[22] Dostoyevsky queried whether the Russian man would be able to cross the borderline. And now, having crossed the line of Christianity, the Russian spontaneity, the Russian elements swept the expanses of Russia. This process naturally ended with the severe dictatorship of Stalin's.

c) THE ELEMENTS – "ALIEN" AND "ONE'S OWN" – AS A PREREQUISITE OF RUSSIAN DESPOTISM

Both the Russian and the German-Roman worlds grew from the explosion of the elements that advanced the legions of barbarians to the Roman Empire in the epoch of migration. The fate of these legions was nevertheless different. The German tribes settled in the area of the Roman Empire, which already had the basis of the European civilization. Slavonic people were pushed Northeast to the region, populated by equally primitive Finnish tribes. As a result, the Slav peoples settled in the area with barren soil while the Germans moved in to the lands which had been cultivated since the times of antiquity, which helped them to get civilized over hundreds of years. This topic was permanent in the reasoning of Russian thinkers about the formation of Russia and Europe.

Nevertheless, both the Slav and the Finnish tribes trod a hard road to the civilized standards of life. Baptism, the Norman invasion which related to young state with the rest of Europe, the contacts with Byzantium, the treasure of antiquities, get Russia involved in the orbit of young European civilizing, though yet partly barbarian, peoples. However, one should take into account the fact that Russia had always been under the impact of nomadic tribes which at that time were at a lower stage of development, living mainly by plunder, i.e.

---

[22] S.N. Bulgakov, *Works*, in two vols., Moscow, 1993, Vol. 2, p. 609.

their culture was parasitic, barbarian. With respect to these tribes Russia
begins to play a part which once was played by Rome and Byzantium with
respect to the surrounding barbarians – the same Germans and Slavs: it repels
their raids, establishes diplomatic relations, Russian princes marry nomadic
princesses... By getting civilized itself Russia tries to civilize its nomadic
neighbours.

But this development was interrupted by a catastrophe. All thinking people
of Russia regarded the Tartar-Mongol invasion of the first half of the 13th
century as a natural calamity. Sweeping all in their way, the hordes of Batu
Khan burnt out and practically destroyed Kievan Rus, leveling down the towns
and churches, killing people and taking them prisoners. The Tartar-Mongol
invasion is regarded as a topical event even today for it was the reason why
Russia became outside of the European civilization space and was pushed
backwards in its development. Land tillage, craftsmanship and trade became
unprofitable because the invaders expropriated any surplus. Since their
domination lasted for several hundred years the civilized life came to a
standstill.

When assessing the destruction of Russia by the Mongol invasion, Russian
historians made comparison with the collapse of the Roman Empire in the
epoch of migration of peoples. N. Karamzin, the Russian historian of the 19th
century wrote: "At that time Russia experienced all troubles the Roman empire
did since the times of Theodosius the Great till the 7th century when the
Northern savage tribes plundered its flourishing areas. The barbarians stick to
the same rules and differ only in strength."[23] No matter how one may respect
Karamzin, the effect and convincing comparisons of his, he shall be argued.
First of all, the barbarians that invaded the areas of the Roman Empire adopted
Christianity, which made a decisive impact on their culture. The Tartars and
Mongols remained alien to Christianity, treating the Church as an instrument,
required for their needs. It is not the Church that subordinated the invaders but,
on the contrary, the invading barbarians subordinated the Church. Secondly,
the German tribes found themselves among the highly developed antique

---

[23] N.M. Karamzin, *The History of the Russian State*, Vols. I-IV, Kaluga, 1993, p. 419 (in
Russian)..

civilization that consolidated for more than one century. Russia had just trodden on the way to civilization. If the Germans appeared in the long run under the influence of Rome they had conquered, the developments in Russia went the other way around: Russia found itself under the strong impact of the Golden Horde that was at lower stage of development. In other words, the yet forming civilization that had no time to consolidate again became barbarian.

A military-tyranic form of government began to establish in Russia. Some historians call it an Asian, Eastern form of despotism. But contrary to the eastern forms of despotism that were quite well in architecture, arts, royal poetry, and had their legislation, the Horde did not have even the rudiments of civilization and civil society. It is only the Khan's cruelty that could hold in obedience the chaotic community that knew no laws. Each member of such a community tried to outdo the Khan in cruelty to serve his favour and benevolence. Lip service to the supreme, treachery if required by the leader, loyalty and readiness to sacrifice one's life for the sake of the Khan who embodies the interests of the state – these are the elements of heritage Moscow got from the Horde. It is these human traits that allowed the Horde and later the Moscow state to become an active and efficient state formation. P. Savitsky wrote that "by way of example, the nomadic conquerors taught Russia to get organized militarily, create the state coercive centre, and attain stability; they imparted a quality to Russia to become a mighty "horde".[24]

Of course, one may not speak in this case about "right" feudalism or about the emergence of the third estate that somewhat reminded the European. Europe was centralized as a result of centripetal tendencies, supported by rich towns and the emerging third estate that learned to become independent, following the example of the feudal state. In turn, Moscow acquired unity by means of the Tartar troops that plundered the towns and principalities that were inimical to Moscow which had a "label of the great principality" from the Golden Horde and which, having deceived the Tartars, consolidated to be able later to oppose them. Moscow managed to rise only because it accepted the functions to represent the invaders, collect the tribute and plunder Russia on behalf of the

---

[24] P.N. Savitsky, "The Steppe and Settled Life", *Eurasia. Historical Outlooks of Russian Emigrants*, Moscow, 1992, p. 75 (in Russian).

Tartars. V. Klyuchevsky wrote that "at first this union was only fiscal, acquiring later a broader basis and becoming political in significance. Being merely a collector of tribute, the Moscow prince was assigned later to be plenipotentiary leader and judge of Russian princes."[25] As G. Fedotov remarked what happened was the "muscovityzation" of Russia or, again in his words, this gave birth to an "Orthodox Khan state". Trying to analyze the origins of Russian Bolshevism and assessing Russia's history from this angle, N. Berdyaev came to the conclusion that the Moscow Orthodox kingdom was a totalitarian state.[26]

L. Gumilev, a sort of herald of the forming anti-legal tendency in Russian social psychology and the present advocate of the Euroasian trend, nevertheless accurately formulates the principle of Russian despotism which was the basis of Moscow Rus. He asserts that the Muscovites "did not try to defend their own rights which they did not have but to receive duties which would bring them the "state remuneration".[27] He holds that it is "this original system of the relations between the authorities and the subordinates so unusual for the West that was so attractive", that it attracted the whole of Russia around Moscow.[28] Given this structure of society, Russia in no way could form civil society, i.e. civilization in the plain sense of the word (from Latin *civilis,* that is civil). In addition, there were no laws, stipulating elementary rights of the individual. "The difference between the estates consisted in duties rather than rights. Each was liable for either defending the state or working to the benefit of the state, that is feed those who defend it. There were commanders, soldiers, workers but no citizens."[29]

Following this thought of Klyuchevsky, we would easily come to the conclusion that if we relax or stop for some reason the absolute power, all components of this mechanism will begin to misfunction (because they lack the element of self-activity) and chaos will set in. It should be added that the

[25] V.O. Klyuchevsky, *Words,* in 9 vols., Moscow, 1988, Vol. II, p. 21 (in Russian).

[26] N.A. Berdyaev, *The Origins and the Essence of Russian Communism,* Moscow, 1990, p. 10 (in Russian).

[27] L.N. Gumilev, *Ancient Rus and the Great Steppe,* Moscow, 1992, p. 624 (in Russian).

[28] Ibidem.

[29] V.O. Klyuchevsky, op. cit., Vol. II, p. 372.

Russian tsar (i.e. king) in the mentality of "muscovityzed" Russia sort of combined the notions of the tsar (i.e. emperor) of Byzantium, being his "successor" as the ruler of an Orthodox state and the tsar (khan) of the Golden Horde. B. Uspensky notes that "in terms of territory, he is the successor of the Tartar Khan but semiotically the successor of the Greek Emperor", the tsar becomes a "more sacral figure than the patriarch"[30] – he is endowed with the divine power by right of birth, that is the state power is more important in Russia than the church power. Therefore, the religious heresies, even such as the schism of the 17th century, could not lead to turmoil, a civil war but the collapse of the dynasty or the relaxation of the tsar power instantly brought about the catastrophic upheavals of the whole nation.

Ivan the Terrible was the last Moscow tsar who terminated the process of formation of the Moscow state independent of the outer enemies (nomadic invaders). However, after the death of his sons and the cessation of his dynasty a time of discord sets in to Russia in the early 17th century. The destructive consequences of this discord can be compared only with the Tartar-Mongol invasion.

The discord of this civil war of the 17th century deranged the whole structure of the Moscow state. Even the election of Mikhail Romanov to the throne in 1613 could not tame the rioting country. It is no accident that the 17th century is called by the historians the "rioting age", i.e. the age of mutinies, uprisings and riots. Russia appeared to a European to be an immense, semi-vacant area with scarce peasant settlements and almost the only major city and stronghold – Moscow. Therefore, riots easily swept the country all over, meeting no obstacle. Here is an abstract of a German thesis, dedicated to the uprising of Stepan Razin (1670-1671) and approved in 1674, that is soon after the uprising: "Our successors would hardly believe that one man occupied such a vast territory over the shortest time and destroyed it to such an extent that over 260 German miles everything was in complete disorder".[31] Europe, too,

---

[30] B.A. Uspensky, "The Tsar and the Imposter; Imposture in Russia as a Cultural and Historical Phenomenon", *Artistic Language in the Middle Ages*, Moscow, 1982, pp. 223, 226 (in Russian).
[31] "Stepan Razin, A Don Kazak, a Traitor." Submitted for public examination, presided by Konrad Samuel Schurzfleisch, speech by Johann Justus Marzius from Mühlhausen, Thüringen,

feared such uprisings: Europeans were afraid that after the defeat of the Moscow government the country might be ruled by a leader who was more tyranic and barbarian and that he would send new hordes to conquer Europe and flood it with a new deluge. However, tsarist Moscow began to accept some forms and standards of the European life and already wanted to be treated as a European country.

According to Russian historians, the essence of this process was in that after the defeat of the Tartars which were the other Steppe the riot was raised by the inner Steppe which did not want to turn to the European urban life with the whole of the country. S. Solovyov estimated this cultural-historical conflict in the following way: "The Steppe... was rising up against the Russian towns, against European Russia".[32] Although these uprisings often had a social character, the nucleus of them was made of Cossacks, that is the layer of Russian people that emerged on the basis of "people" tribute, collected by the Tartars. According to A. Gordeev, an historian of Cossacks people, part of these prisoners, designed to enforce the Mongol army were allowed to settle in the specified areas, have families and their settlement became a military settlement. The armed forces of the Golden Horde were that school that formed Cossacks. Later, over their history, Cossacks were both for and against the Steppe inhabitants, defending Russia's borders but their behaviour was mostly barbarian: they plundered the nearby population of their own kin or alien. For that reason they easily merged with gangsters and other elements, dissatisfied with the obtaining order of things. This was also admitted by the Monarchists who saw in Cossacks a support of the throne.

Russian nihilists realized a robber as a potential revolutionary. For instance, M. Akunin believed that the autocracy was the product of German Europe and saw Russia's "luminous future" in the spontaneous popular social revolution which should be based on "our free Cossacks, numerous tramps... thieves and robbers."[33]

July 29, 1671, *Foreign news about the Uprising by Stepan Razin*, Leningrad, 1975, p. 71 (in Russian).

[32] S.M. Solovyov, *Selected Works, Notes,* Moscow, 1983, p. 147 (in Russian).

[33] M.A. Bakunin, *Philosophy. Sociology. Politics,* Moscow, 1989, p. 541 (in Russian).

The endless riots of the 17th century led to new attempts of the state to consolidate its power by changing the form despotism and allotting the nobility certain rights along with the duties. The state gave them also property, which formerly was only given as remuneration for the services to the state. Formerly all estates had no rights with respect to the state. Now the nobility gained rights over people not only as a tribute for state services but by right of the property owners. People found themselves in new, double slavery now not only on the part of the state but also on the part of private owners. In addition, the nobility became part of the European culture – the fact that separated it from the people even more than before. Citing S. Bulgakov, as regards enlightenment, people remained at the level of Kievan Prince Vladimir. Thus, actually two types of civilization appeared in one country. The Pugachev uprising (1773-1774), although suppressed, wiped out all representatives of the European cultural layer and was an ominous signal that the empire after Peter the Great which left people without rights and property laid ground for the growing contradictions and was fraught with a devastating spontaneous explosion.

The following fact is also essential: the nobility consolidated the state power but did not acquire independence. Since the majority of people remained in the status of slaves, the true civilization did not form in Russia at that time for the nobility, having been a dependent force and fearing the people, remained dependent on the autocracy. What has formed was, in Bakunin's words, a "state civilization".[34] Such a civilization was based on the long run on coercion and despotic power.

At the same time, the socio-economic and cultural principles, incorporated into Russia's economy and culture from the Western civilization, began to shake the solid autocracy, demanding new laws which would provide for the property rights, individual rights and the creation of civil society which naturally was opposite and contrary to the fundamentals of Russian despotism. To a large extent circumstances (the defeat in the Crimean war, reforms of Alexander II) moved the country, as it seemed, Europewise by granting people with rights and opportunities to have property. However, the state feared to give "too many" rights and freedoms and thus relax the state power by waking

---

[34] Ibid., p. 396.

up the spontaneous elements (like Pugachev's uprising). This retarded the reforms in general and the constitutional reforms above all. Possibly, the constitution, if adopted in due time to include all movements and emerging parties, would hold the radical movements, at least their calls to a violent change of the regime. Radicals, even not bloodthirsty, constrained by the absolute autocracy, began to realize that Pugachev's plunderous methods were the prototype of the forthcoming social revolution that might free Russia.

It should be added to the above that people at first realized only the drawbacks of the reforms: the remnants of the serfdom were complemented by the capitalist oppression in the most wild and primitive form. The successes and growth of industry and free enterprise, the flourishing of spiritual creativity became visible later when the epoch, unfortunately, had gone into the past. Some sober minds, like D. Mendeleev (in his analytical work "On the Cognition of Russia," St. Petersburg, 1906) insisted that, if we avoided upheavals, Russia would catch up with the most advanced countries by 1930 but their voices were jammed by the chorus of the most impatient. I shall say that the voice of the Bolsheviks in that chorus was not one of the most loud. All parties hastened the revolution. People cast into oblivion the Russian history, which could have shown that what was needed, was a union of the reformers and the government to ensure the peaceful advance to civilization. But the state failed to meet popular requirements and respond to the reformers.

Today people say that the Bolsheviks cheated on the people and drove them into the camps. Let us see if it is really so. One should not forget that the Russian people, submerged into the marsh of non-historical existence, followed the Bolsheviks. Otherwise they would not win. People had really been driven into the camps and several million people had been subjected to hunger but that was later. The horror of the situation is in that the people at first were waken up and themselves began plundering and destroying the elements of the European civilization in Russia. It was the second time in Russia's history that the spontaneous elements had won (for the first time it was the Tartar elements, for the second our own).

II. Spontaneity's Victory in Revolutionary Russia

In the first years of Perestroika there was no newspaper or other periodical that would not cite "democratic examples" of the Provisional Government, excited by the then Russian freedom and the striving for civilization, and puzzled why the Bolsheviks had won. In short, the period from February to October 1917, was depicted by our Perestroika press as a social ideal which should be followed and that we should get back to it. What was forgotten was the fact that the Bolsheviks had in any case fought democracy and it would not be bad at all to realize in the conditions of overall neurasthenia, threatening to pass into chaos and possible dictatorship, the reasons of the defeat first of the monarchy (already quite European in the 20th century) and then of the democratic coalition of the Provisional Government...

Let us recall that, beginning from the times of Nikolai I, the ideology of unity of the autocracy and the people had already formed. It was right with regard to Moscow Rus. But the rioting 17th century showed that the situation had changed. And the ideological scheme of the Nikolai epoch disclosed how it should be rather than how it was. The growing radical opposition compelled the autocracy to stick to the scheme and live according to the scheme rather than the reality. The illusion of unity gave force to the bodies of power and insurance that they were right. By the early 20th century the contact of the autocracy and the people reached the highest point of illusion. Even desiring to improve the understanding of the people and learn people's points of view, the tsarist government avoided the democratic procedure, which implied a feedback and followed a certain ideological scheme.

In the menacing war and pre-revolutionary years the tsar did not follow with developments, reading the press, or discussing the problems with deputies of the Duma but attended to the view of the "people's representative" (mythical rather than real people) – the famous Grigori Rasputin. His appearance was possible only on the ground of the deep-rooted idea of the "God-bearing people." But Rasputin manifested in himself two sides of the people about which Dostoyevsky wrote: on the one hand, a drunk, pagan element and, on the other, a repenting, wandering subject, confessing his sins to the "old men", the carriers of the Russian Orthodox truth. Rasputin was really, on the one hand, a debauchee and drunkard, and, on the other, an Orthodox old man. History sort of ridiculed the great writer who hoped that the Russian spontaneity could be cured by old men. Right after Rasputin, the "carrier of people's spirit and Orthodoxy", became nearer to the throne, the throne began to shake. Neither the Orthodox Church nor the state could curb the violence of the pagan, popular elements. On the contrary, they sort of encouraged the elements, seeing in them the specifics of the people's spirit: sin and then repentance.

There was a general dissatisfaction with the autocracy that lost ties with the reality and society was unanimous in this. Even the Monarchists and the "Patriots" suggested a national revolution, according to a French ambassador. Of course, the "Patriots" believed that the revolution would run without a riot because the Russian people possessed the greatest source of idealism. But the sober-minded people, and the high-ranking among them, believed that the general dissatisfaction of the educated people with the government was an omen of the looming catastrophe. Maurice Paléologue wrote in his diary on November 13, 1915, the words of a high-ranking Russian officer who said that the Liberals of any kind were "leading us to a revolution which... will carry away themselves in the very first day for it will go much farther than they think; it will surpass all horrors people have ever seen... When a peasant, looking so timid, is let loose he becomes a savage beast. The times of Pugachev will come again... Russian people, the most obedient of all when they are strictly ordered, are incapable of controlling themselves... They need a governor... Maybe this is because of the long Tartar dominance. But that is so."[35]

But such sober minds, which predicted in fact everything, were quite rare. The progressists believed that the people are educated and quite mature for a genuine social revolution and the Patriots were sure that the people was originally "sacred" and was incapable of doing evil. Unfortunately the iron power of the autocracy was orientated towards the same Russian archetype – that of arbitrary rule. The arbitrary rule of the autocratic power, educating even in a small gang of opposition the same propensity to arbitrary rule.

---

[35] Maurice Paléologue, *Au Quai d'Orsay a la veille de la tourmente: Journal, 1913-1914*, Paris, 1947, p. 198.

Dostoyevsky demonstrated in *The Possessed* the striving of Russian Radicals and Nihilists for free manipulation and control over other people's fate.

The autocracy sought a mythological contact with the people, feeling that the people was changing, that the European tendencies were finding their way to more and more people, and that the arbitrariness would not suffice. But the legal structures of civilization only began to form: tsarism did its best to impede their development to its bad luck. People did not know of democratic institutions, they were merely not used to that. Therefore, when the state became weak to restrain the opposition tendencies by force and did not know any other ways of settling conflicts, the explosion went off, supported by society. The spontaneous elements had gone loose, crushing the standards of civilization and those of traditional society. S. Bulgakov was surprised: "The point was in that nobody has ever made a revolution and nobody did not really expect it so soon: it went off by itself, spontaneously."[36]

What happened in Russia in 1917, those "ten days that shook the world" (John Reed) were called, by friend or foe, the socialist or social revolution. The destruction of the former social, economic, state, legal and cultural structures was enormous. The promises and slogans of the new power about building a new, just society sounded too convincing and promising. Undoubtedly, this upheaval also possessed elements of purely social indignation. However, can the revolutionaries' slogan "Rob what was robbed" be a manifestation of the thirst for social justice?

It seemed that the principal defenders of Russian people – the Russian writers – responded most acutely to the catastrophe that swept the country. Regardless of their political bias, the writers and poets assessed the epoch they were living in as the time of apocalypse, finding similarities in the uprising by Stepan Razin and Emelyan Pugachev (poems by S. Esenin, V. Khlebnikov, V. Kamensky and others). Let us dwell on the titles of writings by "red" and "white" writers: "Russia in the Whirl" by A. Remizov, "Russia Washed Up With Blood" by A. Vesely, "Naked Year", B. Pilnyak, "Born by the Storm" by N. Ostrovsky, "Twelve" by A. Block, "Cursed Days" by I. Bunin, "The Kingdom of Anti-Christ" by A. Merezhkovsky, "The Black Book" by Z.

---

[36] S.N. Bulgakov, op. cit., Vol. 2, p. 580.

Gippius, "The Sun of the Dead" by I. Shmelev, "The Road to Calvary" by A. Tolstoy, "God's Scourge" by E. Zamyatin... All these titles bear an imprint of trouble reigned over the country to the detriment of man; birth of the new and death of the old world; moving masses, the new twelve apostles whose spontaneous cruelty helps Block to foresee the Face of Christ – in short, the strain of a cosmic catastrophe is felt in all these titles. Even if one thinks over such a neutral title as *The Cavalry* by I. Babel, he may visualize the hidden sense of the waking trouble. "The Cavalry" implies a task force of the Steppe, nomads and barbarians that again attack the urban civilization. It seems that Babel himself understood the title of his book in this particular way. In his recently published diaries about his participation in Budenny's cavalry this idea is literally worded: "It is not a Marxist revolution, it is a mutiny of Cossacks who want to gain everything, losing nothing. Hatred... to the rich, to the intelligentsia, unfailing hatred".[37]

When Bolsheviks said they were performing a socialist revolution they insisted they did it on behalf of people and at first they were really united with people's spontaneous elements, which they used to gain power. Actually, the October revolution was the first riot in history that had won. Even Maxim Gorky who was close to the Bolsheviks said about the 1917 developments: "I don't see elements of a social revolution in this explosion of zoological instincts. This is Russian riot."[38]

It is no accident that Berdyaev, too, deduced the Bolsheviks' dictatorship from the specifics of Russian history and saw the ideological roots of Russian communism in Russian, rather than European, thought, insisting that the Russian events (revolution, a civil war and the terror that followed) can and should be explained by the Russian realities – a tendency to spontaneity, riot, nihilism, arbitrariness and the like. For several years the country had been reigned by arbitrariness. There were no limits to violence. All was pinned to the revolution and the civil war. At first the Bolsheviks gained by the general destruction of former structures of government, which were capable of rebuffing them. But later, the spontaneous elements began to threaten their own

---

[37] I. Babel, *The Cavalry*, Moscow, 1990, pp. 178-179 (in Russian).
[38] M. Gorky, *Premature Thoughts*, Moscow, 1990, p. 99 (in Russian)

claims to power. The party of destroyers became the party of collectors, in fact claiming the functions of autocracy.

The Bolsheviks' organization was fairly ambivalent. Having emerged underground on the principle of arbitrary attitude to society and the historical process, it was united by iron discipline and could become the framework of a despotic state. It should be added that the Bolsheviks' orientation to violence and arbitrariness was an organizing feature: like once the Tartars did, they collected together disintegrating Russia. The ideas of communism sort of sanctioned violence and justified it for a time in the eyes of Europe.

The spontaneity of public violence was horrible. But the Bolsheviks did not fear cruelty. Today all stories about executions by extraordinary committee without court decisions have been proved with documents. There is a permanent conception that at first Bolsheviks executed only the opposition and representatives of the ruling class. Indeed, during the first years the red terror was aimed that way, given the full approval of people who saw enemy in the intelligentsia and the well-off strata of society. However, one amendment is needed at this point: from the very beginning the Bolsheviks exterminated all who were against their line regardless of their social origin. The degree of their cruelty exceeded the degree of the popular spontaneous cruelty. Violence has been curbed by greater violence. In his recollections Cadet A. Izgoev, arrested in the first year of the new regime, cited a phrase of his pal by the concentration camp in 1918. This phrase explained a lot. Izgoev's counterpart was full of irony to Cadets and other Liberals of the Western orientation but respected Bolsheviks: "It is exactly the government the Russian people needs. Any other government would not cope with it. You think that people respect you (i.e. Cadets). Not at all, they laugh at you and what regards the Bolsheviks they respect them because the Bolsheviks may shoot them any minute."[39]

Instinctively, the new power felt that it should "horrify the people" to use the phrase of Saltykov-Shchedrin. And it did horrify. Like the Tartar-Mongol invaders once did. And later a myth appeared about unity of the party and the people, reminding the old formula of unity of the autocracy, Orthodoxy and people's spirit. The archetype of unity of the people and the power has worked

---

[39] A.S. Izgoev, "Five Years in Soviet Russia", *Life in Lenin's Russia*, London, 1991, p. 72.

to cope with the common enemy – the "bourgeois surrounding." In fact, the Bolsheviks acted against people "for the sake of people" and "in the name of people". For that reason, the robbed people, pushed back from the civilized well being, was nevertheless sure that it was the greatest and happiest people in the world because everything was being done for its sake and the cruelty with respect to itself was regarded as a severe necessity. In other words, slavery gives birth to arbitrariness and the latter again gives slavery. For Stalin's totalitarianism may also be qualified as incessant arbitrariness.

On the one hand, there is no reason to search for the causes of the defeat of Liberal-democratic, "European" tendencies that came to monarchic Russia in the early century bur, on the other, it may be conducive. It may be useful to know whether the mechanisms that triggered off the 1917 riot and let it to the victory are still effective. The reasons for this victory reside in the following.

1. The first factor that caused strain in the country is the social disintegration which was brought about the reforms of Catherine II, the "first Russian privatization" as a result of which a considerable part of people found themselves in slavery and hadn't even tried the relations of private property, had not gone through the experience of owning the private property as the whole of population of Western Europe did. In other words, the major part of people, remaining in the "non-historical existence", did not seek for their rights, the only reaction to oppression being purely destructive.

2. The situation was aggravated by the world war, which required mass mobilization that armed millions of Russians and taught them to kill. The hunger and devastation in the rear regions, shortages of ammunition and munitions in the front, a number of grave war defeats and the animosity towards the government crowned the situation.

3. Military defeats often led Russia to liberalization and political reforms. Usually it took place against the background of the comparatively calm situation in Europe, given no military hostilities. This time the dissatisfaction with the government and the demand of reforms took place during the war and in the situation of a military rage in Europe itself. Europe did not realize the danger of the Russian riot and, on the contrary, it provoked it: what I mean is Germany, which tried to use the contradiction within Russia to its own avail.

4. Russian messianism, which consolidates as a result of the world contradictions of that time, collided particularly in Russia (contradictions typical of the West and the East). Russians believed that Russia would show a way to the whole world.

5. The historical degeneration of the monarchic system of government which manifested itself in that tsarism was unable to suppress the popular riot and the ruling dynasty abdicated at the moment which was most critical for Russia and which left Russia without the only legitimate power in time of war.

6. Ingratiating with people of those who got power in February. This result first of all in the disintegration of the army (order No. 1 allowing to designate commanders by way of election, which turned the army into a gang). Secondly, the permanent calls to expropriate land from landowners without legal decisions of court, in other words, by violence, which deprived the law of any respect of the people. Thirdly, abrogation of the law-enforcement bodies (the police were disbanded already in March, which should symbolize the victory over the "tsarist governors" but in fact it means an onset of robbery and plunder by various dark elements).

7. Coping with all problems by the Provisional Government in a wrong way. The radical issues of the national life were solved by way of decrees which assimilated an idea of arbitrariness in people's consciousness, making the people psychologically ready to the Bolshevik methods and negating the constitution and the law.

8. Illegitimacy of the Provisional Government: a circumstance, which the Provisional Government itself emphasized. As a result, its decrees and instructions might have only a destructive effect.

9. The victory of the Bolsheviks was quite natural because only the dictatorship can rule illegitimately.

* * * * * *

Desiring and foreseeing the collapse of the Bolshevik dictatorship, Russian philosophers abroad were worried at the same time how Russia would survive the new social change. G. Fedotov wrote: "The moment of the communist dictatorship collapse, freeing the national forces of Russia, is at the same time a moment of highest danger".[40] Any collapse of the established way of life, even the hardest one, is fraught with unexpected dangers. What seemed most dangerous was the danger of a new spontaneous riot, which might bring about a new dictatorship. N. Berdyaev wrote about this: "The unexpected collapse of the Soviet power would be even dangerous for Russia, threatening it with anarchy, because there was no organized force which was capable of taking power for creative development rather than counterrevolution".[41] The long-desired collapse has taken place. But it was not the result of a revolution or outside invasion: the regime naturally lived up to its end.

What has happened and is happening in our country? It began with a reshuffle in the central party body which we call today in *apparat* revolution and which the world has recently called "Perestroika." The coup was performed by the top party crust, having particular pragmatic aims. In fact, having lost the "third world war", i.e. the cold war, the top party body decided to sacrifice the ideology of Marxism to gain a compromise with the West. A. Tsipko declared that what was to be blamed was Marxism that came to our country from the West as if Russian thinkers abroad did not know already in the late 1930s that both the Bolsheviks and their opponents Mensheviks were Marxists. But under the cover of fighting Marxism, the party bureaucracy tried to acquire different social, related not only with power functions (which were not long-term) but also with the values which were more solid and long-term and which could be inherited. Under the aegis or democratization and building an economy like the Western, they created a "bureaucratic market".

It would be reasonable to follow the comments of the democratic press which asserts that "Perestroika was initiated and promoted by the top bosses of the party and the state who had, as we know now, quite definite goals: to transfer the shaking political power to more reliable, "democratic" power, the power of capital."[42] Of course, without letting the people to the "second

---

[40] G.P. Fedotov, *The Face of Russia*, Paris, 1988, p. 287.

[41] N.A. Berdyaev, *The Origins and the Essence of Russian Communism*, p. 120.

[42] S. Yakovlev, "Exhausted are the Leaders Rather Than People," *Nezavisimaya gazeta*, March 23, 1993, p. 8.

Russian privatization": they did not intend to divide the state pie into "private pieces".

But "Perestroika" unwillingly involved masses of people and partly acquired a reforming tendency. Let alone the natural desire of people to acquire property. Two movements broke "Perestroika": the separatist movement of the former republics and the democratic movement. Now the democrats are disappointed that the party bosses used democratic slogans to their own avail and spoiled the ideas of democracy, corrupting at the same time some of the democratic leaders. Dissident Lev Timofeev writes "the need of the union with democrats appeared in the minds of the party bosses right after the onset of the reforms. First, they had to find a way to separate themselves without losses from the communist doctrine, which had already been tight for the ruling corporation. Second, the democrats should help them to legitimize their new political strivings."[43] However, democracy became a criterion in assessing the activity of the present leaders. And the majority of them do not stand this criterion. In addition, the ideas of Western democracy were spoiled in public consciousness by the overt corruption of pseudo-democrats.

As a result, public consciousness relates the ideas of democracy and Westernization with corruption, mafia-like tricks of the authorities of any kind, the disintegration of the economy and the decline in the living standards. Naturally, the present developments in our country have little relation to the European principles which imply the modernization of the economy, politics, relations, and above all, open opposition. Meanwhile, we still have too many grounds for worry, dissatisfaction, grim feelings and prophecies. These sentiments explain the success of Zhirinovsky in the last election with his imperial, nationalist programme. It sounds ridiculous to ask questions like this: "Can't people understand that such a choice may lead it to a catastrophe?" The reaction of public consciousness to life hardships, which told on the results of the election, can be understood. I believe that everybody knows today that we will not get back to the old system. Too many irreversible things have happened, which show that the level of spontaneity has dropped. It is this factor

---

[43] L. Timofeev, "Big Waste: Lessons of the Political Defeat of the Democrats," *Izvestia*, February 26, 1993, p. 5.

that impeded so far the consolidation of civilized principles, which allowed developing the spiritual potential of culture and in this sense, the European principles of life.

For that reason, let us try to pay no attention to the relations of the authorities and the former party functionaries, the former dissidents and the "convinced" democrats, communists, nationalists and fascists. All these are but superfluous characteristics of the on going process rather than its essence. If we put aside all words about capitalism that is allegedly forming in this country and that we are getting back to pre-revolutionary Russia, we will see that only one thing really happened: the disintegration of empire, i.e. we entered for the second time after February, 1917, the hardest crisis of a certain structural organization which once stabilizes the mutual relations of heterogeneous, under-civilized elements which have not overcome their spontaneity yet. However, this time the disintegration has no remedy like the international ideology of Marxism, which became a tool for collecting the empire. What is essential is the fact that the crisis is going on in different geopolitical and cultural circumstances. Europe today is not unfriendly to Russia but, on the contrary, it is interested in its stability as a power possessing nuclear weapons and a large number of nuclear power stations. Secondly, there are no domestic cataclysms, which in the beginning of the century went on under the slogan of the struggle between labour and capital. The wars that are going on at the outskirts of the former USSR are triggered off by the domestic problems of the territories that separated.

Both scientists and writers are worried by the disintegration of the traditional structures that kept the empire intact. But this disintegration took place in 1917. And to my mind, the dictatorship of Bolsheviks was a response of archaic society, which tried to postpone its collapse. This was the last emission of the archaic barbarian spontaneity, which had the largest energy potential over the whole history of Russia when the whole layers of traditional Russian society were annihilated. Today we are witnessing the end of this process, which has come to the point at which it began: the disintegration of the empire. One may suppose that, having lived up the horrible epoch of dominance, inimical to the individual – from the explosion of people's sentiments coming into the form of Stalin's terror – Russia was sort of vaccinated for a new kind of spontaneity, getting a chance of building a new type of society unusual to Russia.

It would be naive to say that this process will be easy and promptly bring us to prosperity. We will have less ground to hope that the process will run more smoothly than it did in Europe and we will spend several years to pass the way which Europe covered for centuries. We should not forget that we once tried to deceive ourselves in this way in October 1917. This time the process will be long and unlike the European because our history is different. However, certain things can be predicted from the experience of the Soviet epoch.

This epoch cannot be crossed out from our consciousness – we grew and developed in it. By negating it we would negate ourselves and the possibility of future life of our society, including the possibility of assimilating the European principles understood as free development of creative forces of Russia which originally was a part of Europe to which it is now heading. The specifics of Russian culture fully manifested themselves after Peter the Great returned to the European principles. It is after the Peter rule that Russia became one of the most influential countries in world culture. Even in the Soviet period of Russian history the attitude to the West and Western culture was not utterly negative. By negating the West, we learned from it; cursing it, we borrowed its technology... Even ideology, given the shortcomings of totalitarianism, was orientated towards, Marxism, a European philosophic doctrine. There is a persistent point of view in Russian historiography that, beginning from Peter the Great the introduction into European culture was effected from top. To put it another way, we first built the roof, then the upper stories and the whole building was sort of hanging in the air, having no support in people. The October revolution destroyed these stories and the roof with a mighty strike of spontaneity but the paradox of the post-revolutionary period consisted in that, despite the horrible terror, the fundamentals of Soviet culture were built from the pieces of the culture of European tsarist Russia: education which was an inalienable right of the Soviet people was orientated towards European science and the moral principles were inherited from Russian classic literature, brought up on the ideal of West-European freedom. All this in the long run created a multimillion layer of the Soviet intelligentsia which became a real force in the first years of "Perestroika" which tried to democratize Russia, introduce elements of legal order into the minds of people, reshape the property relations on the legal basis so that the whole of people could experience owning the private property, and the like.

So, what can we say for sure today? The economy is in disarray and society becomes poorer more and more... However, the present disappointment with what is going on testifies that society is capable of criticizing itself (a phenomenon never seen in the Soviet period) and that it is ready to move Europewise. This is our sole guarantee against stagnation or sliding backwards. The very fact that this movement emerged again shows that the originally Russian struggle between the spontaneity and civilization may make a swing in favour of civilization. In any case, the opposite direction of development may lead to a world catastrophe and, therefore, it is useless to discuss it because the nuclear apocalypse is beyond the bounds of historical constructs.

NATIONAL AND STATE INTERESTS OF RUSSIA

Leonid Abalkin*

Turning points in social development are inevitably accompanied by the exacerbation of social contradictions and by greater everyday hardships, and demand that the historical destiny and the future of Russia be considered in a new way. This very painful process of self-knowledge and self-determination is inseparable from revealing and formulating national and state interests, which form the real basis of policies, imparting to them the supreme significance and goal.

National-state, or simply national interests are a key notion of modern political science. As distinct from the West, where large-scale schools exist basing their activities on the analysis of the wealth of historical material and exerting serious influence on mass social consciousness and on the taking of strategic decisions, Russian science has nothing of the kind.

Despite different approaches and methodological principles of analysis in studying that problem its two aspects are clearly seen: the internal one, based on the apprehension of the common nature (from the standpoint of the nation as a whole) of interests of various social strata and groups, on the one hand, and the external one, on the other. Most modern Western researchers focus their attention on the foreign-political aspects of state-national interests. That

* L. Albakin, Academician of RAS; Director of the Institute of Economics, RAS; Editor-in-Chief of the journal *Voprosy ekonomiki*. The article was first published in Russian in the journal *Voprosy ekonomiki*, no. 2, 1994.

national interests are common or conjugated is taken for granted and self-evident. In all probability, this is a distinctive feature of stable and balanced socio-economic systems, as well as the "organic" stages in the historical development of society.[1] Deep traditions of civil society and political culture which make it incumbent on all political forces and movements to follow unfailingly the accepted notions of national-state interests of the country concerned make their imprint here. Otherwise, they would simply be devoid of any chances to have massive backing and influence.

The situation, which we witness today in Russia, is fundamentally different from that described above. Our country goes through the process of radical changes, which do not have any fixed vector. The frames of mind are extremely chaotic and are subject to unscrupulous manipulations. There can be no talk about civil society (in the strict sense of the term) or about a political culture.

This, however, does not relegate the study of national-state interests to the background, making it, on the contrary, very topical. In studying this problem the emphasis should be laid on its internal, not external, aspect, on the awareness of some real common interests, which stand above the interests of various classes, social strata and groups. The common national-state interests do not rule out their multiformity, their internal contradictions, which are sometimes even antagonistic. But it is exactly the common interests that form the basis of civil society, nourishing the policy of social accord. The ability to realize and clearly express these common interests makes it possible to distinguish state wisdom from political adventurism and selfish efforts to promote group interests. The truth of that proposition borne out by age-long

---

[1] In this connection, it would not be amiss to recall A. Bogdanov who distinguished between "organic" and revolutionary epochs. In organic epochs, he wrote "the social world rests firmly on its whales, and these serious, phlegmatic animals, not bothered by sharp harpoons of practical contradictions and ideological criticism, are not inclined to turn from one side to the other... knowing nothing of the accursed problems". (A.A. Bogdanov, *Problems of Socialism. Works Written in Various Years*, Moscow, 1990, p. 77, in Russian). All these problems, which, indisputably, include national-state interests, arise and become sharp and urgent precisely in revolutionary epochs, at turning points of history. Such problems are "a passionate cry of the impotent ethic mentality in the face of a hopelessly prosaic struggle of life" (Ibi., p. 87).

experience has still to be learned by Russian policy-makers and Russian sociologists.

But the real task facing us today is exceedingly more complex. The problem does not boil down to realizing a certain reality, connected with existing common interests. They do exist in actual life, but the ties linking them up are very weakened due to the "rabid" pressure of group egoistic interests.

What we have to do is to mold persistently the very structures of civil society, the solid links - moral, social and legal - which combine various interests, cementing the national-state community of people in line with their interest. It is only in this way that it is possible in some far distant future to overcome apathy, indifference and aloofness, the efforts to survive in isolation, the fear and suspiciousness which are absolutely incompatible with civil society.

As to the awareness and expression of national-state interests, it should be stressed that this process is extremely intricate. We encounter here the indefiniteness and vagueness of the given notion, which was stressed by many investigators and has a bearing on the majority of general notions of political and social sciences. Strictly speaking, the reason for this lies in the complex, many-sided and mobile nature of the phenomena described with the help of such notions. Any attempt at providing a simple definition inevitably results in distorting the essence of the subject matter.

I see the solution of the given problem in studying the objective premises of national-state interests, in revealing their roots and in separating the interests themselves from their outer expression in ideological forms and political doctrines.

It is highly important to stress that national-state interests are inseparable from the entire history of a given country, no matter how old and contradictory it may be, they are inseparable from its culture, traditions, systems of values and the spiritual make-up of its population which were shaping over the ages. "The nation," N. Berydyaev wrote, "comprises not only human generations, but also the stones of churches, palaces and estates, grave stones, ancient manuscripts and books. In order to be able to sense the will of a nation, one has to hear these stones, to read the rotten pages."[2] This applies in full measure to the national-state interests of Russia, which, while being very mobile and mutable – did not arise the moment she was proclaimed independent. History demonstrates that social cataclysms, revolutions or civil wars do not interrupt the connection between times and epochs do not sever the links binding together the country and its people. This is, of course, true, if nations do not perish or leave the historical arena. Such was the case with France and Great Britain, Germany and Italy, China and Japan; such was the case also with the USA from the time of its foundation. The problem of social genes, of a mechanism which provides for the connection of times, the inheritance and continuity in the development of countries and peoples stand in need of an independent study and will not be dealt with at length in my article. Some considerations on that score will be given in its concluding part.

At the same time, although the above problems have not been worked out adequately, it is still important to consider the problems of modern Russia (her national-state interests, in particular) in close touch with her entire history and original culture, her geopolitical position and civilizational peculiarities.[3] This applies to the formation of Russia as a multinational entity which had integrated most diverse peoples and cultures. To a great extent this process is rooted in the political traditions of Byzantium with her ideal of a world empire, capable of preventing the disorderly confrontation of peoples and of introducing a universal peace. True, after the relatively short-lived period, when power was concentrated in the hands of Prince Vladimir and his second son Yaroslav, the Byzantine tradition ceased to be an active political ideology. Division of Kiev Rus into sovereign principalities had prevented the rise of a centralized state with imperial claims for many centuries to come. Modern researchers have conclusively demonstrated the fundamental distinctions of Russia from the other empires known in history and pointed to the formation in her make-up of

---

[2] N. Berdyaev, *The Philosophy of Inequality*, Moscow, 1990, p. 101 (in Russian).

[3] Such a view was organically inherent in our native historical science, it was formulated by S. Solovyev, who insisted that "Russian history should not be divided into separate parts, periods; on the contrary these should be connected and their predominant ties traced, revealing the continuity of forms and principles, considering them in their interaction". (S. Solovyev, *Works,* Book I, Moscow 1988, p. 51, in Russian).

a single multinational superethnos with its own specific features. This fact is not indisputable, but what is beyond doubt is the need to study precisely the national-state interests of Russia, which, in essence, correspond to the notion of "national interests" accepted in Western science. But the literal use of the notion of national interests in the Russian language is ambiguous even for Russia, denoting equally the "national-patriotic" and separatist sentiments.

Another difficulty, which is encountered by practically all investigators of the problem, is the impossibility to explain these interests in a rationalist way. Operating here are some forces, which transcend the frameworks of such an explanation - social feelings and national pride, the memory of the ancestors and the call of the blood. If we ignore the latter, this would not enable science to realize the realities of the modern world and work out an integral concept of social and economic progress. Herein lies one of the manifestations of the crisis of rationalism in modern sociology.

As regards the problem of determining national-state interests, it is a fairly many-sided problem comprising the need to provide favourable conditions for economic prosperity and safeguard national producers, to preserve and improve material, spiritual and moral foundations to the vital activity of a respective social community of people; to discharge functions and duties dictated by the geopolitical position of the country concerned, her place in the system of world economic ties and relations.

The economic component of national-state interests has always and everywhere manifested itself in a most graphic and apparent form. The striving to ensure normal conditions of reproduction, and, subsequently, to strengthen economic might and prosperity, has always been the main spring of the home and foreign policy of the state since it arose. The apprehension of this was first expressed in the naive, but wise formula of I. Pososhkov to the effect that "that state is rich whose people is rich" and then in the ideas of Engels who wrote that "however great and number of despotisms which rose and fell in Persia and India, each was fully aware that above all it was the entrepreneur responsible for the collective maintenance of irrigation throughout the river valleys, without which no agriculture was possible there"[4] . Support and protection of native

---

[4] Frederick Engels, *Anti-Dühring*, Moscow, 1969, p. 215.

producers, farming, industry and trade irrespective of the forms and types of economy, of estate, guild and other group interests, have always been the main component of national-state interests. Later on, development of native science and education began to play a great role as decisive factors of economic success.

Connected with this, consciously or unconsciously, was the apprehension of the evident truth that the might of a state and the welfare of its people are determined, in the long run, by the magnitude of its national wealth (it is no accident that all economists from Adam Smith and Ivan Pososhkov have been writing to this date about the wealth of the people), by the national income produced.

And if we turn to Russia's history, we shall see that the policy of protecting and supporting the producers and merchants was most conspicuous in it. This line can well be traced to the time of the trade route "from Varangians to Greeks", it was realized by the efforts of Novgorod, Tver and Moscow, through the creation, by the Ukaz of Vasily the Third, of the Vasilsursk (Makarievsk, and later Nizhnegorod) Fair, by way of the actions taken by Peter the First to develop manufactures and open up for Russia sea routes, and lastly, through the entire subsequent history of Russia, whose milestones were S. Witte's and P. Stolypin's reforms, the New Economic Policy, the industrialization, and many other major economic steps.

Taxation reforms and the protection of merchants' caravans from robbers, the construction of rail ways and even wars to provide access to rich natural deposits and to the seas and oceans – all this, despite often ostensible motivations, was, in the long run, dictated by the economic determinants of national-state interests.

What we have in mind is not the moral side of the matter or the vindication of particular political actions. This is the more so since all the countries acted in the same way. It is just important to understand that national-state interests have been and continue to be the main driving force of both home and foreign policies. What actually changes is the forms of their protection and promotion, which have since become more "civilized".

What has been said above is connected with the critical review of modern realities in Russia, with the large-scale destruction of her economic and scientific and technological potential, the reasons thereof, and, of course, with the elaboration of a constructive programme of her re-birth as a great power. All steps taken by the authorities, their strategic solutions, all kinds of programmes should not be assessed on the basis of emotions and subjective sympathies, they should be gauged from the standpoint of national-state interests. What we shall obviously need is a more or less adequate institutional form of their expression.

The principle of protecting and supporting national producers does not at all imply the isolation from the world economy or an autarchy. It just presupposes a rational stage-by-stage movement to an open economy, preventing the violation of national-state interests and envisaging a rational use of protectionism. All the developed countries of today have passed through that stage.

Transition from the use of protectionalist measures to the policy of "open doors", and sometimes vice versa, is very instructive from the viewpoint of the mobility and mutability of national-state interests, their dependence on the economic development level of the country concerned and the balance of force in the world trade.

Such changes are usually accompanied by respective theoretical substantiations, preceding the changes in foreign-economic policies or justifying these changes *post factum*.

As distinct from the pragmatically thinking policy-makers, theoreticians are disposed to make absolute of their propositions, considering their formulations as indisputable, as an absolute truth suitable for all times and for all nations. But the specific direction of national-state interests as well as the mechanisms of their realization cannot but change. What is stable in them is the striving to support and protect national producers, production and exchange, as well as national science and education.

As to national producers, these include everybody whose activities are conductive to increasing the country's national wealth and its gross national income produced. Nationality, citizenship or form of owners has nothing to do with this notion. It may be an enterprise fully owned by foreign capital, but working in Russia and working efficiently. It multiplies the economic might of our country and its wealth, increasing (if it exports its output) currency receipts and creating new jobs, helping to solve economic, social and ecological problems through the taxation system.

Therefore, the attraction of foreign capital in the shape of direct private investments (as distinct from loans which not only we, but also our children and even grandchildren would have to repay) meets the national-state interests of Russia.

The complexity of modern of foreign capital in the shape of direct private investments (as distinct from loans which not only we, but also our children and even grandchildren would have to repay) meets the national-state interests of Russia.

The complexity of modern situation consists in the circumstance that Russia faces a number of serious challenges affecting her national-state interests. The disintegration of the Soviet Union entailed various consequences for Russia. In many respects her interests have been dealt a serious and painful blow. In addition to the changed geopolitical situation, very unfavourable for the country and the rupture of economic ties, the national economy was ruined by its worsening structure (a greater share of row materials and extractive industries), by the loss of a considerable part of sea ports, merchant marine and reliable transport routes.

Russia's interests, which were sort of forgotten in the euphoria of destruction, stand in need of a reliable protection. But, to do this, we shall have to take action in new, radically changed and extremely unfavourable conditions.

The weakening of the country and the lack of clear-cut orientations of its leaders have resulted in powerful external pressure being brought to bear upon it. There is nothing unexpected or unpredictable in this pressure. It is a logical result of a strict observance by Western countries of their national-state interests, aimed at protecting and supporting their own business and financial structures. All their actions, including the preservation of limited quotas for Russian exports of goods (with the exception of fuels and raw materials) and technologies (suffice it to recall the unprecedented pressure in connection with the contract for supply of cryogen technologies to India), clearly derive from this simple and logical system. The same equally applies to proposals worked out by Western experts to curtail research in Russia (under the pretext of rationalizing it), especially in most promising areas of science.

What strikes one is the light-mindedness with which persons vested with state powers accept the recommendations of Western experts. They full trust their professional competence (which is often a far cry from being indisputable), their objectivity and disinterestedness. A question naturally arises: we are really aware of what we are doing?

The present-day world, the world economy with its rigorous and powerful laws in particular, is far from being idealistic and altruistic. We should see it as it is, adding or distracting nothing from it. And the sooner we realize its severe realities, the sooner we learn to understand and protect effectively our national-state interests, the nearer will be the aim of the rebirth of Russia.

Lastly, mention should be made of the challenges to national-state interests, which sort of crop up inside the country. What I mean is the predominance in many cases of group and egoistic interests: those of monopolistic groups and some regions, intermediary commercial structures, mafia and management structures, etc. And though this process was in great measure provoked by the mistakes and inconsistencies of the economic policy, it is absolutely impermissible to justify or underestimate its consequences.

And here we must stress once more that to prevent such a challenge is possible only by way of relying on the national-state interests of the country. Only this line of policy can ensure social accord, placing the reform on a reliable foundation and leading to success. This would be a way comprehensible to the people and corresponding to its hopes and aspirations.

Preservation (reproduction) and qualitative improvement of the conditions of vital activities of the existing ethnic community of people, of their gene pool are one of the major factors determining national-state interests. Such factors, which are often relegated to the background in the daily, routine life, emerge at critical junctures (wars, epidemics, natural calamities) as the highest priority, an intransient value, for the sake of which other values and interests can be sacrificed. History abounds in such instances and practically knows of no exceptions. This grants assumptions that the given factor can be considered as a special manifestation of the racial instinct of self-preservation of ethnic groups. This instinct, of course, differs from simple animal instincts; it "dons" social garments and is mediated by social, cultural, political and ideological form. But it does manifest itself as an instinct of self-preservation, conditioned, in the final analysis, by the biosocial nature of Man.[5]

The realization of the given subsystem of national-state interests presupposes protective functions (in relation to external and internal threats) and positive steps designed to improve the conditions of the vital activities of the respective community of people. Furthermore, in both cases it is a question of not only physical existence and material well being, but also of the preservation of and an increase in spiritual values, national culture, democratic principles, the environment and many other things.

Defense of the country, its frontiers, sovereignty and security, concern for citizens living abroad - all this is a specific form of realizing national-state interests. And the extent to which the given functions are discharged consistently and efficiently, may be taken as the yardstick demonstrating the ability of the country and its people to ensure their self-preservation and the correspondence of the country's policy to its basic interests. This equally applies to the inviolability of people's homes, public and private property.

What has been said above is general knowledge. For from time immemorial the need to preserve oneself and survive, to provide for the advance of the ethnic-state community of people underlay the unification of people in civil society, the formation of its institutional structure and statehood.

The crux of the problem under study is that processes have arisen and are gaining momentum in Russia threatening to seriously damage her national-state interests. No main goal in home and foreign policies, failure of the government

---

[5] One cannot but agree with D. Mendeleyev's judgments, who wrote that many investigators "taking into account only individual and social urges and relations, usually leave out of sight the intermediary and extremely important urges to breed and protect their offspring, but it is exactly these urges that determined and will continue to determine not only many important features of individual and social relations, but also many sides of morals and supreme strivings (progress)" (D. Mendeleyev, *To Know Russia*, St. Petersburg, 1906, p. 4, in Russian).

and its bodies to discharge their inherent functions are supplemented by greater individualism, group egoism and separatism, by the striving to solve the urgent problems singly, by one's own efforts. These processes are asocial in their nature and are capable of throwing the country backward, leading it to chaos and anarchy. The fight against the "catastrophe that looms large" makes the need to heed national-state interests all the more significant in order to work out the strategy and tactics of renovating the Russian state.

The new destructive trends have not yet been realized in full measure, but they can cause an irreparable loss for the people of our country. For two years now, the process of the depopulation of Russia has been going on, the death rate exceeding steadily the birth rate. The share of citizens, whose income falls short of the physiological subsistence minimum, is growing. Numerous murders and suicides become daily occurrences. Grave infections are rife and children's health deteriorates. Environmental situation is not improving, affecting adversely the health of people, their capacity for work and intellectual abilities. "Brain drain" is on the uptrend, experts and skilled workers leaving the country.

Taken together, all this deteriorates such an aggregate indicator as the "quality of the population", imperiling the national gene pool.

Some people say that it is not necessary to dramatize the situation. Perhaps, this is true, for politics call for soberness, balanced judgments and impartial calculations. Nor is it necessary to have illusions about the possibility to solve all problems at one stroke. We'll have to climb out of the deepest of abysses in which we have found ourselves.

But responsible politics meeting the national-state interests, must be able to choose priorities, accentuating the most needed actions. Among other urgent problems is the acute need to work out corresponding programmes of saving and strengthening the physical and moral health of the population. Considerable resources should be concentrated here, and their rational use ensured. This must be done even if we would have to reduce allocations for other, also rather important problems, which are not priorities. A society failing to do this has no chance of having its future.

The geopolitical aspect of the problem has a fundamentally different determinant, conditioned by the history of the country, its geographical location, its place in the existing world interaction of states, the operating factors and their counter-balances. Consequently, what we need here is not far-fetched constructions (though the process of learning and forming geopolitical aims may be happy or not, adequate to historical realities or not), what we need is the complex, many-dimensional, objective determination of national-state interests.

Speaking about Russia, we must have in mind her specific features as a great power. This status calls for a complex and contradictory harmonization of her national-state and international interests, the living up to her commitments designed to ensure stability in the world, ecological safety and the survival of humanity.

By and large, the status of Russia as a great power is inseparable from her responsibility (together with the other great powers) for the future of the world community. And this brings about a definite logic in choosing priorities in the economic and social policies, the allocation of resources, including a respective military-political strategy.

Taking advantage of the experience of the past decades and even of more far distant developments, I make so bold as to say that peace is based on a system of particular counter-balances which provide for the balance of forces. Most leading politologists, studying this problem, come to this conclusion. Here we may conventionally adduce the analogy with the balance of forces between legislative, executive and judicial authorities, between government and non-government structures, central and local authorities, and this balance ensuring the effective functioning of civil society. Any upsetting of this balance is fraught with most dangerous tendencies ranging from the establishment of a totalitarian regime to anarchy and lawlessness.

The deranged balance of forces due to the disintegration of the Soviet Union has already now very grave and negative consequences, causing anxiety, especially among the European countries. Other countries are also beginning to apprehend this. The dictate of one super power can seriously destabilize the entire international situation. The restoration of Russia's prestige and influence as a great power meets the interests of the world community, meets her own national-state interests, presupposing certain commitments on her part.

This has nothing to do with nostalgia for the past, wounded pride and selfishness. Russia's discharge of her duties deriving from her geopolitical position is her historical calling, her destiny. History has located Russia as a middle state between West and East, a state, which has absorbed their cultures, systems of values, civilizational peculiarities. It has largely been and can be in even greater measure a bridge connecting these two different worlds, contributing to their better mutual understanding and their mutual spiritual and moral enrichment. This, of course, calls for the rejection of primitive and, at the same time, very dangerous attempts to look for some ideal model of the social and political system, culture and religion. It calls for the recognition of the laws governing the multiform models of the social, economic and spiritual development of countries and peoples belonging to the particular types of civilization.

The history of Russia and her geopolitical position have conditioned a rather particular correlation between the state and the individual, between collectivist and personal principles, economic rationalism and spirituality. Gained over the ages and transmitted through the channels of social memory, these aspects remain even today the inalienable and unavoidable features of her social and economic image, her system of values and motivations. To lose sight of this means to try and stop the movement of history. Such a policy is incompatible with the true, profound national-state interests of Russia.

The geopolitical position of Russia objectively calls for a many-sided orientation of her foreign policy, her organic incorporation into all the enclaves of the world economy. Any attempts to make her relations with one country or a group of countries the corner-stone of her foreign policy, runs counter to her national-state interests. Many-sided orientation is a strategic principle and it must not be violated under any political circumstances or pressures.

We must not even raise the issue of the priority relations with a particular region – be it near foreign countries, the former CMEA member-countries, the South-Asian countries, China or the USA. Many other countries may, evidently, have geopolitical priorities, but not Russia as a great power. I believe that it is this approach that should underlie our global and everyday foreign political activities, defining the structure of the respective departments, research work and the training of personnel.

The actual problem is that the above factors are realized or not, that the realization of a historical mission by a particular country does never proceed smoothly, meeting with no resistance, but always in struggle. Such are the laws of political life.

It would be very instructive to trace the historical road traveled by the Russian state revealing how its basic foreign policy was pursued in most diverse conditions and under most diverse regimes, how, lastly, despite the growing resistance and bitter defeats, the country returned time and again to its historical road. If some people dislike calling it its historical fate, let it be calling, predestination, the geopolitical logic or a law-governed regularity.

The role played by Russia has always given rise to apprehensions and even fear in the West. They feared her. We have to admit frankly that representatives of our glorious Motherland provided, unfortunately, quite a few reasons for such judgments, nourishing the strivings to humiliate and weaken Russia.

This state of affairs is characteristic of the present time and of the past. N. Danilevsky wrote with bitterness about the inconsistent and insidious policy of West European countries in relation to Russia and her national-state interests.[6] Kerensky wrote in detail about the plans of dismembering the Russian state at the end of the First World War in his memoirs, which were recently published in this country. He cites numerous documents, which, in his words, preceded the "Versailles tragedy". Among them are US commentaries envisaging the recognition *de-facto* the governments representing Finns, Estonians, Lithuanians and Ukrainians; treatment of the Caucasus as the sphere of influence of the Turkish empire, the granting to some power of a limited mandate to govern Central Asia on the basis of the protectorate, and, lastly, creating of "fairly representative" governments for Great Russia and Siberia.[7]

In a word, actual historical processes and the role of the state determined by its geopolitical position, can hardly be described in no uncertain terms.

---

[6] N. Ya. Danilevsky, *Russia and Europe,* Moscow, 1991 (in Russian).
[7] A.F. Kerensky, *Russia at the Turning Point. Memoirs,* Moscow, 1993, p. 372 (in Russian).

Forces of a different scale operate here tantamount by their strength to tectonic forces.

There is no doubt that radical changes have occurred in social development, especially in the latter half of the present century. New possibilities have been opened up, changes are on hand to regulate relations between states on a basis, which is fundamentally the role of Russia may assume a new image determined by her geopolitical position.

We only wish that these chances were not missed. But at the same time, we should not leave out of sight the fact that politics remains a stern matter, pre-set rigidly by national-state interests. One must not sit back here indulging in wishful thinking. Smiles and embraces must not deceive the realistically thinking policy-makers irrespective of their orientation.

In the system of international relations, the state comes forward as the sole and potentiary representative of national-state interests, expressing and protecting them.

In the internal life of the country, the matter is much more complex. The state is equally called upon to express the common interests of the people and it discharges this function, as a rule, the better and more efficiently, the more democratic and law-abiding its system is. Such an approach to the role of the state rules out its consideration only as a tool of a class rule. The functions of the state were discussed theoretically and methodologically as far back as the 1960s and the 1970s when two aspects of state activities were singled out the state as a tool of a class rule and as an agent expressing the common interests of all classes and social groups, their interaction and integrity.

If the last circumstance: enables us to regard the state as an integral component of the mechanism of representing the common interests, its class nature makes it possible to understand why the state cannot be the only mouthpiece of national-state interests. The fight for power has always been and continues to be an arena of the sharpest political struggle. And each party or public movement, striving for power, explains its claims to power by the fact that it can express common interests better than others.

As a rule, in this succeed parties (movements) which express the interests of those classes and social groups, which, at the given stage, coincide in the greatest measure with national-state interests of the country, the complete coincidence being hardly possible.

And here we should make, at least, two conclusions. First, an effective realization of national-state interests does not presuppose the monopoly of one party, it rather presupposes a specific system of forces of containment and counter-balances, a guaranteed recognition of the rights of the minority, open democratic control over all branches of authority, in a word, it presupposes everything that constitutes the characteristics of the rule-of-law state. Secondly, a reliable representation of national-state interests demands that all institutions of civil society be "actuated".

We shall not deal with this problem at length, considering only one, exceptionally important circumstance, which is not always taken into account. As we have said above, different parties and movements claim to express national-state interests. But who is the arbiter to settle their claims? And are there objective criteria enabling one to assess the programmes and slogans offered to society with the help of certain scale of values?

Evidently, there is no such scale. As to the supreme arbiter, the people always play that role as the supreme sovereign of the democratically organized society. But this essentially correct answer hardly reveals the real mechanism of the people's sovereignty, all the more so if we take into account the large-scale manipulations with public opinion.

Solution of the problem evidently lies in the analysis of value orientations and ideological aims inherent in the given society. The latter accumulate the age-long experience, sometimes the intuitive, subconscious assimilation of national-state interests. In forming them a tremendous role is played by the spiritual culture of society, its historical traditions, a system of confessions, people's legends and heroic epos. The memories of the great past, pride for the deeds of one's ancestors, not only forms national-state interests, but if also gives birth to a powerful energy of creation and progress.

Today, attempts are made to avoid these issues under the slogan of deideologization, to sever the nexus connecting modern Russian society with its history. In this context, it would not be amiss to stress that the historically shaped political and ideological values are not mere inventions, peculiarities inherent in our country alone. They are universal characteristics, most strikingly manifested in countries with highly efficient and dynamically developing economy and stable social and political structures.

To illustrate this we may refer to the analysis of the 500-year period of the development of America given in the *International Journal of Social Sciences*. Its first issue in Russian has been published recently. In particular, it mentions that the integrity and self-identification of North-American society have taken shape on the basis of the recognition by various social groups of the "basic political and ideological prerequisites of American civilization". Incidentally, this was the reason why it failed to integrate the Indian population with its "insurmountably original self-identification, absolutely alien to new ideological frameworks, laying claims to its own, independent integrity". As to the political and ideological aims as such, these emphasized individualism, personal achievements, republican freedoms, anti-state pathos (hence the extremely weak development of the concept and the ideology of the state as distinct from the ideology of the people and the republic), recognition of the quasi-sacred status of the economic sphere.[8]

Institutionalization of these indefinite, very vague qualities of the "people's spirit" is usually connected with the formation of various structures in the sphere of religion, culture, science and education.[9] In some cases, they may be supplemented by more or less formalized government and non-government structures engaged in working out the concepts of national development and in strategic planning. They sort of accumulate, keep and express the respective values and principles, which, subconsciously but indisputably determine the very type of national mentality, as well as the choice of problems and the type of decision-making in political and economic activities.

In this subtle and very delicate sphere, it would be naive to count on the artificial implantation of new values and aims, which do not rest on the basic foundation of social self-consciousness. Here the processes go slowly out of

---

[8] S. Isenstadt, "Culture, Religion and Development in North American and Latin American Civilizations", *International Journal of Social Sciences*, 1993, No. 1, pp. 181, 186, 191.

[9] "Like water seeping into soil, it is exactly culture that unobtrusively molds Man's world, creating the character of the entire nation" (Daisaku Ikeda, *The Rebirth of Humanism*, Tokio, Soka Gakkai International, p. 40).

sight, which does not, however, imply that the intellectual elite of Russian society – the custodians of national-state interests – refuses to fulfill its duties and moral obligations. In a broader sense, representation of national-state interests is inseparable from the formation of civil society and its institutions.

The great significance of national-state interests for the historical fate of the country, the people makes it necessary to consider any threat to these interests as an issue of national (state) security. Such an approach renders it possible to build up a reliable system of state security, deliminating the spheres of activities of the respective structures and bodies. Under certain circumstances, not only the defense of the country, but also the fight against the environmental challenges, against criminal-mafia groups, the salvation of the genetic fund may become and actually do become the issues of the national-state security.

The moment the threat to national-state interests emerges, group interests and political ambitions should be relegated to the background. The entire might of the state establishment and all the forces of civil society must enter the struggle. As the history (both of this country and of the world) demonstrates only on this road success can be reached. All other roads lead to the ruin of the state, making efforts of all the preceding generations meaningless.

Realization of these historical lessons is called upon to become a lodestar both in studying the problems of national-state interests of Russia and in political actions designed to protect and realize them.

POLITICAL CULTURE OF RUSSIA: CONTINUITY OF EPOCHS

Dmitry Gudimenko[*]

A s we know, the political behaviour of citizens is influenced not only directly by their views and convictions, political sympathies and antipathies, but also and rather often by their subconscious stereotypes and habits determined by their social milieu and transmitted from generation to generation. For that reason, in analyzing the modern political processes in Russia and in trying to forecast their further development, we constantly come across the problem of a *political culture*, i.e., a totality of political norms, rules, principles and customs which are accepted (officially and non-officially) in the country and which set rather strict limits (often unobtrusively) to the possibilities of statesmen and rank-and-file citizens in both drafting programmes and in implementing them. Willy-nilly, a political culture turns out to be that foundation on which the edifice of real politics rests. And if the plans of a particular policy-maker come into collision with the political culture of the people, they are unfailingly rejected by the popular masses or are distorted to an unrecognizable degree in the process of their implementation. To understand the distinctive features of the political culture of Russia and to study its evolution in the period of the dismantling of totalitarianism is especially important both from the theoretical and practical standpoints.

[*] D. Gudimenko, Cand. Sc. (Hist.), Institute of World Economy and International Relations, RAS. The article was first published in Russian in the journal *Polish*, No. 2, 1994.

Today, we can say for sure that the real results of the policy pursued in Russia after the fall of the communist regime, proved to be very far from what had been expected of them, dissipating numerous hopes. The rise of new forms of life had encountered a host of problems which complicated the internal political situation: the ever growing economic crisis, the conflict between the various branches of power, chaos in the sphere of constitutional legislation, confusion in relations between the Centre and the regions, stronger separatist trends, growing scale of corruption and crime, whose levels approximate those of the time of the civil war. And all this is largely determined by initial political mistakes which from the start failed to take into account the rather striking peculiarities of Russia, her historical, national-cultural and socio-economic and even psychological originality.

Of first-rate significance is the circumstance that the origin and present-day actual state of Russia's political culture gives one no grounds to call it a liberal-democratic one, it can be rather listed among the authoritarian-collectivist political cultures responsible for the specificity of political processes in our country.

Since the mid-19th century a tradition has been formed in our historical and philosophical literature to explain the peculiarities of Russia's political development by her natural-climatic and geographical factors, there being a surprising unanimity on that score of "occidentalists" and "adherents of one's own native soil". A most clear-cut expression of that concept is to be found in L. Gumilev's thesis about the irresistible power of the isotherm of January which divided the population of Europe in the West European (Roman-German, Protestant-Catholic) and Russian (Orthodox) superethnoses. There is no denying that this proposition has certain grounds.

Modernized and systematized, the theory of climatic and geopolitical determinism is expounded in a recently published book by A. Fonotov, who provides a very original concept of the historical road traveled by Russia. Generalizing various date about the dynamics and peculiarities of socio-economic and political processes in Russia over ages, the author arrives at the conclusion that they had determined a *mobilization type* of the development of our country, which he describes as "the development oriented on the achievement of extraordinary aims, using extraordinary means and extraordinary organization forms." Such kind of development, Fonotov points out, was favoured by complex natural and climatic conditions and a constant threat on the part of her outside adversaries. Owing to this, Russian society had always to exert all-out efforts in the fight for survival, subordinating personal interests to the interests of the state and setting limits to the personal freedom of its members. And the larger-scale of the threat to the existence of society is, "the higher are the demands on the state, on its abilities to give an adequate answer to challenges, the more severely have to act the subjects of the state establishment and the advocates of state interests. As a result, the entire functioning of society is subjugated to the accomplishment of this main task", concludes A. Fonotov.[1] In other words, the "catching-up" development to which Russia had been fated since the time of Tartar-Mongolian invasion, called for the need constantly to "spur" the course of natural developments, forming ramified mechanisms of extra-economic coercion and the respective norms of political behavior.

Of interest is that investigator's conclusion to the effect that Russia has a definite socio-economic genotype, which influences the course of political and socio-economic processes and the forms of relations between the individual and the state. Extrapolating this judgment to the sphere of political culture we have good grounds to say that Russia possesses a specific *political-cultural* genotype.

As many investigators suppose the Russian civilization is a "daughter" civilization in relation to the Byzantine; at any rate, it may be assumed tat the Byzantine tradition had been a system-forming factor of the Russian history. The cultural (including the political-cultural) continued connection of Russia with Byzantium one may see in the inheritance of the specific imperial idea of the state. Secondly, Russia inherited from Byzantium the role of the buffer and middleman between east and West, with political-cultural orientations to tolerance and the striving to synthesize the achievements of Europe and Asia. And, thirdly, among the characteristics inherited from the Eastern Roman

---

[1] A.G. Fonotov, Russia: from Mobilization Society to an Innovational One, Moscow, 1993, p. 83 (in Russian).

Empire mention should be made of cosmopolitanism or oecumenicalism, the supraethnic, the supranational character of power and statehood, as well as the "internationalist" approach to forming political and intellectual *elite*. A. Toynbee defined that characteristic of "East-Christian" civilization as the striving to create a universal state and a universal church and combine them.[2]

The unique feature of Russia is the interruptory nature of her history. On its historical road, she has passed through the following stages of cultural and political development: 1) the heathen period; 2) Kiev Rus of the Christian time; 3) the Moscow tsardom; 4) Petersburg empire; 5) the Communist period; 6) the present-day post-communist period. Each successive historical stage denounced in a revolutionary way the preceding one and - at great sacrifices - it rejected not only some or other forms of political and social organization, but also the former rules and values. It is only natural that it was not only shortcomings and organic defects that were rejected, but also some achievements gained in the preceding period. But no matter how sharp and even cruel the way of parting with the past could be, at all the stages of development some fundamental characteristics of preceding periods were spontaneously integrated. Owing to this, the political culture of Russia has displayed the surprising stability of its basic characteristics, its structures. For that reason, we may speak of some viable, traditional foundations ("constants") of the political culture of our country, which stem from the Russian national character and the peculiarities of the historical development of Russia; all the changes notwithstanding, these characteristics are transmitted from one generation to another, being differently "arranged", but preserving its essence practically intact. Considering these "constants" of the political culture of Russia we are able to make certain conclusions.

Irrespective of changing regimes and democratic and non-democratic procedures, power in Russia is traditionally of the autocratic character. Autocratism (in its "mild" or "rigid" form) permeates, as a rule, all public and government structures from top to bottom, determining the character of their functioning. Political ideas of the population are based on the spontaneous monarchism ("leaderism"); correspondingly, the political system is always and

---

[2] A. Toynbee, *A Study of History*, Vol. I, London, 1954, p. 29.

actually built on monarchic or quasimonarchic principles, though the "monarch" himself may be the heir-at-law or may be elected for the term of his life or provisionally; he may bear different titles: Grand Duke, Tsar, Emperor, General Secretary or President. Furthermore, the "monarchic" system is invariably reproduced both globally and locally. It was already M. Lomonosov who compared the history of Russian and Roman empires, using formal criteria and pointing to the following dissimilarities: "The Roman state was elevated by a civil rule, autocracy caused its downfall. On the contrary, non-conformist freedoms practically ruined Russia; autocracy first elevated her, and, after some unhappy times, multiplied, strengthened and glorified her"[3] In these words the sad truth corroborated by our entire history is expressed, demonstrating that Russia is constantly faced with two threats - tyranny or anarchy. An authoritarian political-cultural matrix of our country channels Russia's development in one of the following three regimes:

1. *Stagnation* (typical of it is the rule of Nikolai the First and L. Brezhnev). Characteristically, it cannot boast of any significant achievements, but it does not equally have any sharp flops. This is a time when the government slackens the reins, not using it to "rear" the country. The people relax after the period of constant tensions, but during the lost decades the ballast of social vices is amassed unnoticeably. In so doing stagnation tends to develop into the "regime" of catastrophic ineffectiveness.

2. *Catastrophic ineffectiveness* (political fragmentation on the eve and at the time of the Tartar-Mongolian invasion, the beginning of the reign of Peter the Great, the region of Nikolai the Second etc.) - periods when weaker authoritative principles result in the terrible and often disgraceful defeats.

3. *Catastrophic effectiveness* (the reign of Peter the Great and the rule of J. Stalin, to some extent, the reign of Ivan the Terrible) - the surmounting of the ineffectiveness of the preceding "regimes" at the cost of tremendous overstrains, frantic efforts, numberless victims and unheard-of hardships. The political form of the "regime" of catastrophic effectiveness is the "developing dictatorship", which forcibly interrupts the tranquil slumber of the country and

---

[3] M. Lomonosov, "Ancient Russian History", *Russia and Europe: an Experiment of a "Councillist" Analysis,* Moscow, 1992, pp. 21-22 (in Russian).

modernizes it by inhuman, often even barbarous methods. It may be said that the need for Russia to catch up with more developed countries fated her to vacillate from catastrophic effectiveness to catastrophic ineffectiveness, with dangerous stagnation in between.

The style of interrelations between society and the state, indirectly expressed in citizens' attitude to the state and the attitude of the state to its citizens is the most important aspect of political culture. On the strength of some historical circumstances, the state invariably holds a dominant position in Russia's social life. For many centuries on end it has not been the state that grew from civil society, the latter developing under a rigorous patronage of the state, which has always been (and continues to be) the "prime mover" of the development of society, initiating all substantial transformations. Democratic rights and freedoms were not, as a rule, won by society, they were granted by the grace of the monarch. Perestroika, which historically should be regarded as a bourgeois revolution, was launched by the leading *elite*, not the popular masses. Transition to democracy was proclaimed by leaders of not a democratic Party. It may be said that etatism is inherent in the social life of Russia: the state holds the dominant position, while society is subordinated to it; this accounts for the unequal relations between the state and the individual. What we have, then, is as follows:

1) immense political role of bureaucracy;

2) paternalism and clientelism (patronage by the state, by some of its bodies and officials; use by the *elite* of predominantly non-formal connections): a person counts on social promotion resulting not from his personal work contribution (the Protestant model), but strives to gain a higher ladder in the state hierarchy, availing himself of respective benefits and privileges;

3) "exclusion" of broad popular masses from the everyday political process, a limited sphere of public political activity and consequently, a massive political inertia;

4) no civilized (or, at least, correct) forms of interaction between the "top" and "low" layers, legislative nihilism, which regularly results in revolutionary and counter-revolutionary outbursts at the "top" and at the "bottom". Citizens' mentality is marked by the combination of a complex of being a loyal subject

and a complex of being a revolutionary. Using the words of A. Pushkin in his novel *The Captain's Daughter*, all revolutions from "below" tend to develop into "a Russian riot, meaningless and ruthless."

N. Berdyaev, was perhaps, the first to stress the paradoxical nature of the political culture of Russia. He pointed to the duality and irrationalism of the "Russian soul" – a striking symbiosis of anarchism and etatism; willingness to give one's life for freedom and servility; chauvinism and internationalism; humanism and cruelty; asceticism and hedonism; "angel's holiness" and "brutal wretchedness". Berdyaev saw the reason for this in the underdeveloped state of principles of individualism in Russian society, in spontaneous collectivism. Besides, he voiced a supposition about the "feminine" nature of the Russian people when the state is seen as a "masculine" principle, i.e. as something external, shaping and channeling uncontrollable people's element into definite frameworks. This thesis (possibly most disputable) may be taken as a "working hypothesis" describing figuratively, but rather adequately the character of interrelations between the state and society in Russia. As a result of it and as distinct from Western Europe, Russia had the state of a different type – a state that molded society.

L. Tikhomirov was right when he said that the people's mentality divides state power into "supreme" and "executive" (administrative) power[4]. And if the "executive" power may, depending on specific circumstances, be structuralized rather intricately, from the supreme power the people demands simplicity, homogeneity and clearness. It may be said that Russia is willing to recognize power, which to one extent or another is of sacral character. The concrete manifestation of this can be seen in the fact that people in Russia do not, as a rule, demand from the supreme ruler the "effectiveness" in the pragmatic sense of the word, addressing their claims to various intermediary instances. The main function of the first person, the leader (Tsar, General Secretary, President) is to play the role of the supreme arbiter, the guarantor of law and order, and his power is explained by the presence of charisma and the striving to achieve ideologically motivated absolute ideal, not by rational logical reason, nor by his victory in party struggles. Etatism, hypertrophy of the state and the

---

[4] L. Tikhomirov, *Monarchic Statehood*, St. Petersburg, 1992, pp. 46-47 (in Russian).

atrophy of civil society, the almost complete subordination of the former to the latter, condition Russia's such feature as the lack of her own *social* integrating foundations, a very weak ability of the people of *self-organization* which is especially manifested at the time of crises. In the periods of political cataclysms when the state disintegrates and fails to discharge its functions, Russian inhabitants display a surprising helplessness.

The etatist nature of the political culture of Russia results in that the notions of patriotism and loyalty to the regime, love of one's Homeland and his subjects' love of power are mixed up in people's mind. Because of this the patriotically thinking men usually fail to distance themselves from unpopular governments and to come forward as an independent force, being fully confused when revolutionary-reformist forces come to power (this is exemplified by the complete insolvency of conservatives in 1917 and the passivity of "patriotic adherents of the state" in the end of the 1980s and the early 1990s). For their part, radicals of the democratic kind insist on radical changes and often denounce patriotism as a sign of reactionary moods and even as an inclination of fascism.

Using Toynbee's terminology, we may speak of the *futurism* of the political culture of Russia – of its projection (perhaps, illusory) into the future and of an insufficient attention to the past without a *conscious* observance of traditions (the unconscious observance indisputably takes place), of an extreme ability of taking over new departures (which usually come from the West). The vision of the future, of course, changes, depending on a particular epoch. An assumption may be granted that futurism is based on the non-acceptance of the vices of the real, existing society, which have always been too many in Russia. It stands to reason that the thesis about the futurism of the Russian political culture should not be understood literally; futurist projects determining the countenance of a particular epoch inevitably harbour certain archaic elements. This absolutely applies to the project of Peter the Great; the communist project has also demonstrated a striking combination of futurism and archaism. Especially characteristic in this respect is the example of late Stalinism, which consciously and purposefully cultivated certain archaic elements connected with the symbols and the ideology of the Petersburg empire (golden shoulder-straps for officer, invocation of old military traditions, strict ranking of bureaucracy, the "ampir" style in architecture, flirting with the Orthodox Church and a wide use of Rusophil lexicology in official propaganda, the fight against the kowtowing to foreign experience of all kinds and indoctrination of state patriotism). The moment the *futurism* potential of a specific model grows weaker or proves to be exhausted, the next model immediately succeeds it. Thus communism succeeded the Empire, and was itself succeeded by post-Soviet democracy.

If we accept the thesis about the futurist political culture of Russia, we can then explain such paradoxical, at first glance, fact that it was exactly the Brezhnev period – most favourable period in the Soviet history in terms of "cheap" and "abundant" food, when our compatriots forgot what hunger meant and when alongside "party meetings," "socialist emulation movement" and "lessons of politics", such new attributes of the "Soviet way of life" appear as telephones, TV sets and comfortable one-family apartments – that proved to be times of sharp frustrations and disappointments. At the same time in Stalin's epoch unprecedented sacrifices and hardships, hard labour and even bloody repressions were taken for granted, bordering on emotional upsurges and euphoria. But as the "epoch-making feats" were replaced by the routine and drudgery work which more often than not brought no tangible results, as daring attacks gave place to routine operations, and as increasingly smaller room was left in everyday life for sacrifices and heroism, social realities entered into increasingly sharper conflict with the cultural "matrix" of the people which rejected grey *routinism*.

The political-cultural "pallet" of society in Russia is characterized by extreme heterogeneity, by the existence of various subcultures with absolutely different, if not diametrically opposite, value orientations, their interrelations being confrontational, if not antagonistic. If we have a look at the political history of Russia in the past three centuries, it will not be hard to notice constant conflict of subcultures – occidentalist and Slavophile ones; radical and patriarchal-conservative; archaic and etatist, and nowadays of "democratic" and "communist" subcultures. What is more, the last period over a century and a half, have been marked by the existence of active, often aggressive and fairly numerous counter-elite which mobilized and accumulated the potential of social and political protest, striving to topple the elite and take its place.

By and large, what is characteristic of the political culture of Russia is practically *no basic consensus*, no national accord, but, on the contrary, a painful strife between social groups. The differences between subcultures are often so striking, that one may get the impression that individual nations exist in Russia, united only by common language and common area.

Inasmuch as this or that model of the future is usually built on a definite vision of the past, and the past of Russia is so contradictory and many-faceted, that its unambiguous treatment is impossible, it is only natural that the sharpness of our political and philosophical controversies should often reach a critical point. When regimes change and people come to power with a different understanding of the tasks facing the country and a different vision of the future, history is ruthlessly re-written. For that reason, the witty persons christened Russia a country "with an unpredictable past". Sharp conflicts, the "barricade mentality", latent non-acceptance of pluralism, the striving of many political subjects to hegemony and unification of world outlooks – all this is a striking peculiarity of the culture of Russia which has left an indelible imprint on the style of political life and the character of relations between the state and the individual. The "limited political space" and the desire of the ruling forces to occupy it wholly results in the existence of the constructive opposition being practically impossible; at the same time opposition manifests itself either in the shape of timid law-abiding desire to "eliminate individual shortcomings" of the system, or in the shape of a tough anti-system line.

Inherent in Russia is a great-power (supra-national) idea of "humane" imperialism, which goes, depending on different regimes, through various metamorphoses. In the Russian mentality the state also predominates; not the national self-identification of citizens; the national factor is often marginal, while the state and the majority of the population are tolerant nationally and religiously (evidence of it can be seen in the light manner in which Russians marry persons of different nationalities and different races). Things being like this, the imperial consciousness combines in a paradoxical way with internationalism, while patriotism is, as a rule, of a political, not a nationalist character. Let us recall that it was already Kiev Rus that had been built on a polytechnic basis – it comprised on an equal footing not only the Slavic, but also the Baltic, Ugro-Finnish and some Turk tribes, which fact in advance ruled out all ethnocracy. Russia had always been (the Soviet years included), a unique, the only one of its kind, empire in which the "colonies" enjoyed privileges and advantages at the expense of the "mother country". The word "Russian" denoted in pre-revolutionary times "an orthodox subject of the Russian Empire", i.e., it was ideological and political category, not an ethnic one. With the passage of time the pre-revolutionary fact of "being Russian" readily turned into the fact of the post-revolutionary "being Soviet" and subsequently into the "fact of belonging to Russia". As a result of this, it is hard for Russians to identify, formulate and defend their own national and ethnic interest. F. Dostoyevsky pointed more than a century ago to an "extraversy" of our country which lacked an egoistic approach to formulating its own (foreign) political priorities.[5] This is connected fairly closely with the circumstance that the Russian national idea is marked by Messianism (in its varying hypostases), altruism at the national level, insuppressible desire to show humanity the road to happiness, as well "idealism" ("antimaterialism" and "selflessness"). This trait of the political culture manifested itself, perhaps, most strikingly in the Soviet time.

Berdyaev believed that two conflicting forces constantly collide in the psychics of the Russian – natural heathishness and orthodoxic asceticism, aspiration for the other word. Berdyaev wrote: "The religious formation of the Russian soul has produced certain stable qualities: dogmatism, asceticism, the ability to suffer and sacrifice in behalf of its faith, whatever it may be, striving for transcendentalism which relates now to the other world, now to the future and this world". Further on he pointed out the concrete manifestations of these qualities, which, in our view, are of fundamental significance: the religious energy of the Russian soul is capable of switching and heading towards goals which are no longer religious, for one, towards social goals. On the strength of

---

[5] F. Dostoyevsky, "A Writer's Diary for 1822", *Russia and Europe: an Experiment of a "Councillist" Analysis*, p. 79.

the religious-dogmatic frame of their souls, Russians are either orthodox or heretics, sectarians; they are apocalyptics or nihilists.[6]

Thus, Marxism, which in the West was a purely scientific theory to be criticized and examined rationally, turned in Russia into a variety of religious revelations. The skeptic criticism of Westerners is alien to Russians, and this invariable results in shifts and substitutes, concludes Berdyaev.

What is most important in that for ages on end Orthodoxy a Russia held the position of *monoideology*, being the backbone of the national culture? Ideological monism underlying the political culture of Russia remained fully intact even after religion had lost its former role and a secular society had emerged. After 1917, communist ideology and propaganda took over in many respects the role and the functions of religion, creating a sort of an atheistic cult with its priests, saints and holly books.

The outer manifestations of the collapse of the Communist regime which we have been witnessing since 1991, are far from testifying to an easy transition from totalitarianism to democracy, because this transition implies not only the creation of democratic institutions and structures of civil society, but also the overcoming the habits, the way of life and the style of thinking that have taken shape over the years, it implies the rooting out of the totalitarian political culture.

And what matters here is not only the inertia, which keeps afloat the outdated stereotypes. Our position is complicated by the fact that in Russia communism was not an infection brought in from outside. On the contrary, it was in a sense the quintessence of the "mobilization type of development", and, at once, the logical consequence of the typical traits of the Russian national character. Totalitarian [residual effects" would prove more viable in our country than in other countries which have freed themselves from the communist rule. It is apparent that the pronouncements of "the architects of Perestroika" about the transition to democracy were dictated not by their personal democratic convictions and sympathies, but rather by the obvious economic and ideological bankruptcy of communism and also by the decay of

---

[6] N. Berdyaev, *Sources and Meaning of Russian Communism,* Moscow, 1990, p. 9 (in Russian).

communist culture. And this is a reason why at this stage of the development of political culture these elements of decay prove to be very strong, often overshadowing and even suppressing the need of forming democratic culture proper and preventing the establishment of the sound norms of political behaviour. As a result, Russia of today has many political and cultural features in common with Thermidorian France: a feverish re-distribution of the national wealth, the atmosphere of the troublesome time, the urgent striving to grasp as much as possible, the "mentality of time-serving" based on the covert motto: "After us, the deluge" corruption, cynicism and baseness. And it is likely that these negative traits will long be poisoning the political atmosphere in Russia.

The political culture of modern post-communist Russia is still something indefinite and contradictory. After ideological pluralism was "legalized" in the end of the eighties, it soon became clear that the elimination of the political-cultural heterogeneity in the communist period was illusionary. It may be said, that, on the one hand, the struggle (now overt, now covert) is going on with varying success of opposite political trends (democracy – authoritarianism, centralization – regionalization, globalization – isolationism); we see the confrontation of perfectly different subcultures (communist, radical-liberal, national-patriotic), whose representatives use so dissimilar political languages and resort to so different systems of political argumentation due to their peculiar frames of mind, that it is likely that they hardly understand each other. On the other hand, a narrow legal political spectrum after the events of October 3-4, 1993, which seem to have removed from the political arena a number of radical oppositional organizations, induces the opponents of the government to pass from the anti-system opposition to intra-system opposition (i.e., the struggle in the framework of the market economy and Presidential Republic).

The realization is growing among the ruling quarters that Russia is unable to enter the "common European home" immediately, where nobody waits for her. If the importance of defending of state interests and of taking into account its national specific features is properly understood, then there is a hope that Russian political culture would be consolidated on some compromise footing. The present-day situation confronts the investigators with such questions as, evidently, nobody is in a position to answer. It is still not clear which would prove to be stronger – the deep-rooted totalitarian stereotypes or the effects of their untenability and discrediting. The effect of discrediting the officially declared communist values which stem from the parasitation of the communist values which stem from the parasitation of the communist system on the ideas of patriotism and selfless devotion, on the distortion and vulgarization of all lofty principles began to manifest itself in the poles of good and evil changing places in the minds of many people. Thus, a transition took place from the complete non-acceptance of capitalism with all its attributes to the rupturous imitation of it, copying, and apologizing for everything that constitutes its real vices. Unemployment, speculation, the cult of money, economic licentiousness are today treated as fully sound phenomena, while many regard civil equality, social justice, altruism, patriotism and spirituality as something obsolete, almost indecent, while selfless enthusiasm is practically considered to be a symptom of feeble-mindedness.

The communist society had, undoubtedly, ridded itself from the most crying social contrasts, but it had lost, in the process, a considerable part of its cultural and intellectual potential, accumulated by the educated layers of pre-revolutionary Russia. Destruction of the old cultural elite, the "aristocracy of the spirit" brought about the degradation of the population; the mediocre standards, mediocrity began to reign generally. What is more, the inadequate process of modernization of Russia and super fast, inorganic formation in Soviet years of higher social groups gave rise to such a paradoxical phenomenon as the *non-elitarian elite*, its plebeian character. (If we examine the social structure of communist Russia from the standpoint of consumption and proprietary relations a conclusion may be made that a certain "middle class" had practically played the role of the elite, whereas the absolute majority of the population was removed to the position of the "lower class".) A prolonged estrangement of the people from property and the decision-making process had inevitably given birth to lumpen-proletarian mentality literally among all layers of society, which, in turn, creates today an extreme instability of social moods, profused promises and a high susceptibility of demogogism.

Mention should also be made of such a specific feature inherited by Russia from the USSR as the "colossal durability of technostructures, whose hyperdevelopment had long been compensating for the absence of legal institutions of civil society plus the situation with the *elite* and culture"[7]. This circumstance is objectively conductive to the preservation of administration-command, not political principles of governing the country, the state and the economy and, consequently, to the preservation of the power of the "old cadres" – nomenclature workers and technocrats as the most proficient experts in this sphere. The atmosphere of "Regional Party Committees" persists in the corridors of power, where the political process, to use W. Churchill's figure of speech, represents the battle of bulldogs under the carpet. And on top of it is an another circumstance: 70 under the carpet. And on top of it is another circumstances: 70 years of a totalitarian rule conditioned the excessive growth of the re-distribution mechanisms, where it was not money as symbol of the results of the distribution of social wealth, but an actual access to the leverage of distribution - political power – have acquired first-rate significance. In the present-day situation power readily "converts" into money, while money without power means very little. In modern Russia the relationship between etatist and antietatist moods, between activism and escapism, radicalism and conservatism is far from being unambiguous, confounded largely by existing contradictions. The question arises of possible (permitted by political culture) forms of political mobilization, structuralizing and expressing various interests. The sad irony of our situation consists in that the transition to multi-party system in our country took place at a time when in the developed world the classical model of (multi) party mechanism experiences a serious crisis. And if in Western Europe the stability of party systems is supported by deep traditions and political inertia, in Russia, where practically all parties arose from scratch, the process of forming multi-party system founds itself, I believe, in conflict with the spirit of the time.

As a result, reviewing the position of parties in modern Russia we arrive at a striking conclusion. In post-communist Russia parties hold in public opinion (and, consequently, in social life) a clearly peripheral position. The illusory nature of party activities can be clearly seen, since the course of the real

---

[7] M. Malyutin, A. Yusupovsky, *Alignment of Political Forces in Russia and Their Role in the Near Perspective*, Moscow, 1993, p. 4 (in Russian).

political process is determined by non-formal groups with the dominating position of the state and state bureaucracy remaining intact. Incidentally, this can be easily explained: the extent of the structuralization of society (which, as is known, does not boil down to the differentiation by income levels) and which is needed to secure an adequate party system as well as the realization by social groups of their own interest are still very insignificant. Regional socio-economic heterogeneity of our society and the instability (due to an accelerated transition to a new social system) of frontiers between various layers, call in question the possibility of establishing "class" ("Estate", "professional") parties. Thus, the catastrophic failures at the elections of December 12, 1993 of parties which openly declared as their aim the promotion of interests of definite social layers was no accident – in particular the Party of Economic Freedom (the "Party of the exchange dealers") and the Civil Union (the "Party of Directors"). On the other hand, the ideological factor in conditions of total skepticism, faithlessness and disappointment due to the collapse of communism and economic crisis can neither play an integrating role in forming parties. In this respect Russia of today resembles Germany after 1945. Deideologization is a product of the dismantling of totalitarianism, and it takes time (at least several years) to fill the ideological vacuum with some stable and systematized positive ideas. As the electoral campaign of December 1993, showed, all electoral blocs and alliances took great pains to avoid recourse to ideological arguments.

Essentially we live *not so much under the multi-party system as under a proto-party* (if not *non-party* system) this being a distinctive feature of the political culture of Russia.

In the long run, the problem of the evolution of the political culture of Russia may be reduced to the following: would our country be able to build up a stable democratic system and enter in a dignified way the third millennium or would the burden of authoritarian-monarchic and totalitarian traditions outweigh, pushing Russia back to where it had been before. And it is not at all the question of whether formal democratic procedures can be introduced into the political practice or not – this gives rise to no doubts whatsoever. The actual issue is different: can civilized and organic relations between Man and the State be attained in Russia, when citizens would really be in a position to influence the policies of the authorities, while the state would cease to be a self-sufficient bureaucratic corporation or a tool to satisfy somebody's selfish interests, turning into a conductor and protector of commonwealth, a totality of institutions provided society with favourable possibilities for development? Would Russia be able at least to overcome the chronic irresponsibility of political leaders, irradicating a situation where the powers that be are not controlled by society, making the government discharge its functions competently. Let us hope Russia will be able to do this.

THE PROBLEM OF OCCIDENTOPHILISM: TODAY'S OUTLOOK

Alexander Volodin[*]

Nowadays our prospect for future have really become the talk of the town. People suggest numerous forecasts and predictions, substantiated one way or another, but few took the liberty to assess the responses to such questions as "Where is the history heading?", "What is to become of the country (culture, philosophy)?", especially n the conditions when there are no objective parameters of the country's movement. To some extent the situation may be elucidated by a retrospective analysis of what the country was in the past and from where it is moving.

A. Herzen said that "...by looking back now and then we see our past from a different angle and inspect in it a new side, adding to our knowledge of the past new experiences. By improving our knowledge of the past, we understand the present better; by plunging deeper into the past, we expose the essence of the future; looking back, we move forward".[1]

It is known that the past is likely to prophesy. We inquest the past and if we possess the faculty for putting the right questions it will inevitably steer us to the right way. The more so, the past can make "hints" with regard to the future conveying them through our consciousness to mold it in a certain way.

[*] A. Volodin, D.Sc.(Philos.), Professor of the Russian Academy of Management. The article was first published in Russian in the journal *Svobodnaya mysl* nos. 7-8, 1994

The topic "Russia's Fates" is eternal in our culture. This is especially true since the time when the thinkers of national brand, unengaged in the political regime, did their best to mold a complex spiritual creation which we now call national consciousness (not to be mixed with state self-consciousness). There were times when this topic became prominent to oust all the rest to the background. Naturally, this was most manifest at times of wars and other social upheavals. Nevertheless, it was often the topic of hot dispute in "peaceful times", too, especially of the philosophic and historical character.

The 1840s were one of such periods when the best representatives of the national intelligentsia initiated a dispute between the so-called Western and Slavophile trends of thinking. It is exactly that time that gave birth to such notions as Occidentophilism and Slavophilism although these notions were rather far from the actual essence of each trend.

Our present life is oversaturated with linguistically non-committed words, which are often very far from what the speaker implies. If Francis Bacon were still alive, he would possibly derided the proponents of the phantom of communism or those who earnestly try to invoke the spirit of capitalism as a new idol. He would undoubtedly have said that they are possessed with the idols of the Market (the Square) rather than the idols of the Theatre. To put it another way, they are fully dominated by words. He would have remarked that we command a richer vocabulary compared with his contemporaries but not because we are smarted or more learned but merely because we give names to non-existing things even though related with reality. He would have defined such words as "confused and ill-defined, and rashly and irregularly abstracted from things"[2] .

It seems to me that the names of the latter origin also include the words Occidentophilism and Slavophilism. However, given the evident laxity of meaning, each of them hides the might of tradition and habit.

One will easily notice that these words are quite different, each having its own flavour and colour. Slavophilism invokes an image of Russian birches and the national beverage, called "kvas". It sort of irradiates glory and love while

---

[1] A.I. Herzen, *Collected Words* in 30 vols, Moscow, 1954-1960, Vol. 1, p. 824 (in Russian).
[2] F. Bacon, *The Novum Organon*, Oxford, 1855.

Occidentophilism is associated for many with something alien, decadent and fraught with disintegration.

Isn't it a wonder that everyone can cite a range of literary pieces, old and new, dedicated to Slavophiles, while hardly anyone is likely to recall a book, treating of the phenomenon of Occidentophilism? Evidently, this phenomenon has deeper reasons than the differing quality of the names per se.

It would be pertinent to cite a consideration by P. Annenkov, a participant in the dispute of the 1840s: "The epithets, given by both parties to each other were not quite accurate: Moscow and Petersburg, Slavophile and Occidentophile... Inaccuracies of this kind are unavoidable in any case if the dispute does not predicate on the real ground and is carried out using other methods and arguments than required. Whatever has been said about the Occidentophiles, they have never rejected the historical conditions which specifically define the civilization of each nation while the Slavophiles allowed any imputation when they were accused of being inclined to stationary forms of reasoning in science and art."[3]

The very Annenkov admitted, and one can agree with him, that the ideological collision of these two trends in national thought turned to be a difficult and contradictory process which promoted the formation of national consciousness, identified various types of the approach to the problem of "inner sense of the Russian history", to the "place Russia occupies among the European nations, and to the methods of self-education and self-determination which we should select to make this place honourable in any respect." According to Annenkov the point was in "determining the maxima of morality and beliefs and in creating the political programme for the future development of the state", in preparing future "reforms and changes".[4]

Many issues of the dispute were "sublated" by reforms of the government of Alexander II in the 1860s-1870s. Yet, right before the reforms began, newspapers and thinkers of different ideological orientation definitely voiced their point of view that the issues of former opposition had been exhausted. For instance, *Otechestvenniye zapiski* wrote in 1859 in this respect: "Sooner or

---

[3] P. Annenkov, *Literary Recollections*, Moscow, 1960, pp. 215-216 (in Russian).
[4] A.I. Herzen, op. cit., pp. 217, 215.

later each term becomes exhausted and loses the meaning it formerly implied. The same goes for Slavophilism, too". It has almost no sense now as a term. The same transformations took place with regard to so-called Occidentophilism, too: the both parties originated from the bounds limited to them by our literature and became not quite sensible, if one judges them by their names. Now we can note that today some Occidentophiles are closer to the Slavophiles than to themselves and this fact is the result of our literary activity of the past five years, which is a best proof of the progress in science and literature.[5]

Nevertheless, years later up till now some scholars try to identify the main core of all ideological and political struggles in Russia in the confrontation of Occidentophilism and Slavophilism. Some allege now that the inability of these political forces to come to an agreement motivated the victory of the Bolsheviks in the early 20th century, and that at the end of the century Occidentophilism is embodied by Academician A. Sakharov and Slavophilism by A. Solzhenitsyn.

I would like to draw attention to one peculiar feature of modern political games, which is not quite harmless to Russian society, which is too excited even without them. It became fashionable to identify in Russian political life two extremely contradictory points of view, which allegedly stem from Slavophilism and Occidentophilism. Russian political scientist A. Tsipko defines them in the following way: "On the one hand, it is nationalism and patriotism which discard democracy, regarding this as an inevitable phenomenon, and, on the other, it is a conviction that democracy is possible without patriotism"[6]. Actually, American historian A. Yanov who emigrated from the USSR may find the same in the writings. When asked whether he was sure that the Western way of development was better suited for Russia, Yanov said: "I recently talked about that with Baburin. He is not against democracy, but he reckons that it should be combined with patriotism. However, the Russian idea, which makes the basis of this political stand, cannot be tied with democracy. It rests on the Utopian idea of universal consensus, while democracy implies that there are irreconcilable interests in society. It predicates

---

[5] *Otechestvenniye zapiski*, 1859, December, Dept. III, *Russian Literature*, p. 121.
[6] *Znamya*, 1992, No. 1, p. 187.

on the idea of opposition. In fact, it is no more than an effective mechanism of reconciling such interests. The Russian idea is deprived of such a mechanism. Therefore, in critical situations it degenerates into dictatorship, autocracy, fascism."[7]

Although such inferences reflect a dangerous differentiation of opposing social forces in our society they are nevertheless distorted to my mind. Their authors actually deprive democracy of any Russian trait, identifying democracy with Occidentophilism, and depriving the other side of democratism.

Nevertheless, despite the widely accepted prejudice, the founders of Occidentophilism were no less patriots than Slavophiles. Merely they were patriots of "another kind". In 1864 Herzen responded to Slavophile A. Samarin, accusing Herzen of the lack of patriotism: "Our love [to Russian people – A.V.] is not only a physiological perception of tribal affinity, based merely on the accidental place of birth; this love is above all united with our strivings and ideals, it is justified by belief and reason and, therefore, it is easily accepted, running in tune with the activity of the whole life".[8] In their turn, the founders of Slavophilism, opposing the "stagnant West", used in their constructs many things, borrowed from the Western social and intellectual experience.

V. Solovyev emphasized that the Occidentophile point of view is far from excluding the national originality but on the contrary it requires that this originality be manifested in full.[9]

But let us get back to our time. The trouble is that the "identification" of modern Russian through the past is often effectuated in theoretically senseless, and practically fruitless (if not harmful), forms of historical romanticism of any kind which is in the particular case the type ignoring the reality of restoring ideological consciousness.

The representatives of a form of that kind posit a problem of Russian national consciousness and solve it in a very peculiar way: by calling for the "spiritual renaissance of Great Russia", they attempt to neutralize the

---

[7] *Nezavisimaya gazeta*, February 20, 1992.

[8] A.I. Herzen, op. cit., ol. 18, p. 276.

[9] V. Solovyev, "Occidentophiles, Occidentophilism", *Encyclopaedic Dictionary* by F.A.

Occidentophile democratic ideological heritage, in fact, to abrogate the essential layer of national intellectual culture of the 19th century. For instance, by identifying the Russian culture with Orthodoxy and Russia's history with the imperial statehood, some authors withdraw the whole of Occidentophilism beyond the bounds of Russian culture and philosophy; they regard the deeds of the Occidentophiles as the general discrediting of the Motherland's reputation, as "drop-outs of arrogant anti-culture", a "noxious potion of the Western mystic and anti-Orthodoxy".

This trend of "national patriotism" is often manifest in today's newspapers in its extremely aggressive embodiment. One step more and Mikhail Lermontov will be ousted of the Russian culture – Lermontov who called Russia a "country of slaves, a country of segniors" in which "people" is obedient to the "blue uniform", Alexander Pushkin may also share the fates of Lermontov for saying once: "It's the devil ploy to be born in Russia, should and talent alike". And naturally Leo Tolstoy will surely side with them for dishonoring the Orthodox Church, serving the autocracy.

* * * * * *

I would single out three basic ideas, introduced into the national culture by the 19th century Occidentophilism.

The first idea may shortly be formulated in the following way: the Occidentophiles insisted that Russia should be inherent in the context of the world, primarily European history, depending in its development on that context (rejecting at the same time the idea of Orthodox Russian Messianism which was typical of the Slavophiles and which was the product of idealizing certain social and spiritual features of Russia prior to the Peter the Great period).

Here is, for one, the point of view of Nikolai Chernyshevsky: "Everybody knows that for many years our fate has been related with the fate of Western Europe and each major event there has repercussions on us. Friedrich II robbed Maria Theresia and we got entangled in the Seven Years' War. Europe began

---

Brockhaus and Efron, Vol. 12 (23), St. Petersburg, 1894, p. 244 (in Russian).

to extol Voltaire and we initiated a comedy of humane utterances to please Voltaire, hypocritically exalting our liberalism, although Voltaire had a lot of true advocates in Russia. The French Revolution broke and the character of administration in Russia became more resolute and direct, exposing their philosophic decorations. The Revolution brought about Bonaparte and we got entangled in protracted wars that ended successfully, joining Warsaw to Russia but devastating it in the long run. Then Metternich founded in the Holy Alliance and who does not know its impact on Russia? The list can be continued. But it seems that the cited facts are enough to utterly reject the mere possibility of light-mindedly regarding the West-European developments".[10] Chernyshevsky believes that "Russia's situation cannot be understood without analyzing the processes in the West, both past and present.

In addition, I would like to cite an article by P. Lavrov (1864) which is unknown to the modern reader. In his article "From the Editor" Lavrov who edited the *Zagranichny vestnik* (News from Abroad) holds that the "Russian issues, Russian necessities and even general issues from the Russian point of view came to the foreground in Russia literature". Lavrov definitely claims that "Russian society is still in need of the results of the European thought. One can hardly admit that Russians, secluded in their own interests, should remain alien to what is going on in Europe. The majority of the Russian reading society follows the European developments with great attention and interest and cannot afford to alienate itself from the European life." Further he emphasized that this is merely out of place. "Equally, he goes on, it would be unwise and even harmful to literally copy anything that is alien like it would be equally harmful to utterly reject everything that is alien because it is alien. The diversity of tribal and historical situation is subordinated to the same universal laws of human life, which have an impact on the development of our country, too. Refusing to study the laws' manifestations in most diverse forms which admit of their accurate investigation we deprive ourselves of studying the laws which govern the social life of our own."[11]

---

[10] N.G. Chernyshevsky, *Selected Philosophical Works*, in 3 vols., Vol. 2, Moscow, 1950, p. 636 (in Russian).

[11] P. Lavrov, "From the Editor", *Zagranichnyi vestnik*, 1864, No. 1, p. 1.

However, this passage calls for serious reservations.

Admitting the common laws of human development did not mean that the Occidentophiles unambiguously recognized as mandatory the historical route of the Roman-German nations and negated the specific features of Russia's development. One way or another, the Occidentophiles admitted the fact of Russia's backwardness, that Russia belatedly joined the universal civilization, having no solid organic traditions of national development.

This partly explains the numerous statements of Herzen about the "Russian people being young" and the "chaotic state of social relations in Russia" as compared with the European situation which "has settled to be quite consolidated and right-minded".[12]

Other thinkers also made similar declarations and comparisons. For instance, N. Mikhailovsky saw the Russian specificity in that even in the second half of the 19th century Russia didn't have "any definite" social ethical traditions. Speaking about the "mishmash" so typical of Russia's social and spiritual life and about the "lack of any history", Mikhailovsky wrote that in the West "history is the basis of power, firmness and certainty but it guides that power in a diverse way which may be right or not, for one hand, and, for the second, it creates a cumbersome tradition which precludes the freedom of critical spirit. The lack of history [in Russia – A.V.] is the reason for flabby ethic but at the same time if a country devoid of history gives birth to a personality, endowed with the instinct of truth, this personality is capable of greater courage and endeavor than the European man because he is not dominated by history and the grueling pressure of tradition." According to Mikhailovsky, the Russian man had no reason to stick to the "social partitions [that is to the rigid differentiation to social classes - A.V.] which had never been erected by our history with the European certainty and stability."[13]

But insisting on the Russian specificity of Russia, Mikhailovsky, like other Occidentophiles, utterly rejected attempts to identify their basis in any specific, original Russian spirit. Differentiating between the notions of "nation" and

---

[12] A.I. Herzen, op. cit., Vol. 14, p. 170.

[13] N.K. Mikhailovsky, *Works*, in 6 vols., Vol. 3, St.-Petersburg, 1888, p. 159 (in Russian).

"people", he staunchly rejected nationalism, criticizing for that reason the Slavophile ideas in any manifestation.

Let us now dwell on the *second* merit of the Occidentophiles. It is known that all constructs of the Slovophiles are pivoted on the mythologized conceptions of the community as a social personality in which each individual on his own will refuses from himself, freely subordinating himself to the communal being.[14] They subject themselves to an equally mythologized conception of love as an allegedly basic prerequisite of typically Slavonic (Russian) morality and in this connection, Orthodox Christianity as a religion which corresponds to the spirit of the Russian people. The principal socioethical value of the Occidentophiles was the personality, its liberation from traditional, mainly patriarchal and medieval, tangles, proclamation of its liberty and self-value and development of its activity in history.

This was also the basis of the Occidentophiles' patriotism, directed towards the future of the Motherland, rather than the past or present, the principal trends of inner history of the Motherland "expressing the necessity to call the personality for activity and living, and introduce it into the general economy of development."[15] These are the words by Kavelin, written in 1884. He voiced similar ideas in the 1840s, too.

In his article, "An Outlook on the Juridical Life of Ancient Russia" in which V. Belinsky identified the fundamentals of the "philosophic study" of our history when speaking about the development of German tribes which made the basis of the European life and about the states, created by them, Kavelin asserted that these states conducted gradual "education of man". "The thought of its absolute merit passes gradually from the domain of religion into the secular world and begins to be accomplished in it... Numerous private unions are replaced in them [various states - A.V.] with one common union whose goal is all-round development of man, his education and support of moral dignity... Our Russian-Slavonic tribes had... no beginning of the personality. The household relations were incapable of breeding in a Russian Slav a feeling of

---

[14] Yu. Samarin, *Works*, in 10 vols., Vol. 1, Moscow, 1890, p. 63 (in Russian).
[15] K.D. Kavelin, *Our Mental Structure. Articles on the Philosophy of Russian History and Culture,* Moscow, 1989, p. 289 (in Russian).

originality and concentration which makes man to draw a distinct line between himself and the others, and always and everywhere distinguish himself from the others... Here man plunges into dreamy moral serenity. He is credulous, weak and carefree as a baby. The profound feeling of the personality is utterly out of place. Such existence without the beginning of personality is impossible for people called to act in the new world... The degrees of the development of personality and the corresponding degrees of decay determine the periods and epochs of Russia's history."[16]

Other outstanding Russian thinkers held similar points of view. "...We do not accept anything in the universe higher than the human personality," wrote N. Chernyshevsky, being convinced (and persistently convincing his contemporaries) that "the necessity of individual activity is the principal feature of the present situation" in Russia.[17]

Herzen most explicitly expressed the same dogma of the Occidentophiles: "The freedom of the individual is the greatest matter; it is only freedom that can produce the real will of the people. The individual himself should respect his freedom and pay tribute to it no less than in his kin and the whole of the people."[18]

These words explicitly express the creed of the Occidentophile trend of Russian thought. But it is important that one should pay attention to the context in which these words are said. By substantiating his decision with these words to remain in the West where "a lot of human has been elaborated despite the external order and the official system", the author compares Western Europe with his Motherland: "Even in the worse times of the European history we encounter certain respect for the individual, a certain recognition of independence: certain rights given to the talent and genius. Despite the vileness of the then German governments, Spinoza was not exiled; Lessing was not flogged or recruited to the army. This is not only the respect for the material and moral power: this involuntary recognition of the personality is one of the great human principles of the European life.

---

[16] Ibid., pp. 22-23.

[17] N.G. Chernyshevsky, op. cit., Vol. 2, pp. 582-583.

[18] A.I. Herzen, op. cit., Vol. 6, p. 14.

Nobody who resided abroad or moved into America has never been regarded a criminal or traitor.

The matters are quite different in our country. The individual has always been subjugated and depressed, never trying to voice anything in his favour. A free word was regarded in our country as impudence, originality as sedition; the individual got lost in the state, dissolved in the community... Slavery rose with education; the state grew and improved but the individual gained nothing; on the contrary, the stronger the state, the weaker the individual."[19]

These and similar provisions made a fairly stable ideological foundation of the Occidentophile philosophy and in particular the basis for critique of various forms of pseudo-collectivism which neutralizes the personal fundamentals, both in historical realities and the Utopian social doctrines (various forms of barracks communism).

It should be admitted that the very notion of the individual and its freedom was not understood equally by all Occidentophiles. Some of them shared, or pretended to, the concept of individualism which was very popular in the West but often was met with critique from European anthropology (e.g. Ludwig Feuerbach and young Karl Marx) and a number of national thinkers who managed to rigidly differentiate between the idea of "narrow egoism" (individualism) and the idea of "free individual" that cannot develop without developing simultaneously the relations and the feeling of "solidarity". The anthropological doctrines of A. Herzen and P. Lavrov are most illustrative in this sense.

Lastly, the "third" aspect of the Occidentophile heritage which deserves to be mentioned. It is particularly Occidentophilism that posited the important problem of the legal support of the individual freedom, which was traditionally neglected in Russia, emphasizing the significance of the legal aspect in the provision of the individual freedom and the necessity to legalize the human rights.

---

[19] Ibid., p. 15.

In due time, Chaadaev complained in his "Philosophical Letters" that Russia didn't even have "an elementary civil code – the political and juridical ABC which we encounter in all Western peoples."[20]

Calling Russia a "grievous kingdom of lawlessness," Herzen wrote in the late 1850s: "In fact, the idea of law hardly exists in Russia: it is mixed with the recognition of power or the accomplished fact. For us the law has no other sense except the prohibition of the powers that be; we do not respect the law but, rather, fear the district policeman... We do not have those accomplished notions, those civil verities which the West uses as a shield to defend itself from the royal power and now from social ideas..."[21]

The juridical thought of Russia had gone a long, hard way of evolution, meeting with the opposition of both the government conservatism and the conservative traditions of "society" and even the people. Nevertheless, the 1870s-1980s gave birth to an idea that it was necessary to establish an order in the country, which would be based on the precise, mandatory law. The liberal Occidentophiles.22 principally brought up the best national lawyers the idea the best national lawyers and students of state were from that medium.

* * * * * *

Leaving aside the issue of the objective heterogeneity of the Occidentophiles, the disputes within this trend about the ways of Russia's Westernization, I will only note that the spiritual capital, accumulated by the Occidentophiles during the whole period of existence of this trend will appear to be more topical and fruitful than the romanticized and philosophized "national patriotism" of various kinds, taken as a variety of the conception of originality (to which we can refer Slavophilism, too).

National patriotism, insisting on a special Russian way, rested one way or another on various myths, based mainly on the allegedly God-given "Russian soul" or "Russian idea", dictating a national sense of life, mission, function and other constants. This also includes the conceptions about original Orthodoxy,

---

[20] A.I. Herzen, op. cit., Vol. 14, p. 168.
[21] Ibid., p. 169.

people's morality, based on love, and the like as genuinely Russian attributes and the initial fundamentals for solving the "Russian question". Slavophilism as a social doctrine was *historically justified and theoretically valuable* because it kept alive those realities which allowed its founders to ideologize and mythologize them (among the founders were such figures as I. Kireevsky and A. Khomyakov, Yu. Samarin and K. Aksakov, et al.). This went on as far as the patriarchal peasant community and Orthodox religion were deeply rooted in people's minds.

The fact that the Slavophile Utopia rested on these realities explains why some Occidentophiles (e.g. V. Kavelin) recognized certain "truth" in Slavophilism and even some of them turned to Slavophilism, which testifies that the borders between these "trends" were rather flexible. In this case I may remind the reader Herzen's "Russian socialism", the zeal of Chernyshevsky when he defended the peasant commune in 1858-1859, and in general point out to the ideology of populism in the broad sense of the word.

Nowadays, the peasant commune totally abrogated by the Soviet power, and the Orthodox religion do not any longer make the core of the people's consciousness. Despite all attempts to reanimate it, it is mainly a form spiritual compensation in our society, which is becoming apathetic to it or regards it as variety of fashion.

Whatever our attitude may be to the present situation, the permanent, dramatic reality is that the country is sliding through the barbarous market to a regime where everything would be allegedly ruled by private property. However, this advance to the "world civilization, is going on in conditions of total degradation of the population, to put it plainly. The country has hardly any middle class of which dreamt most of the Occidentophiles in the middle of the past century. We have no classes with their own mentality and culture. The recent talks by "scientific Communists" about social homogeneity of the Soviet society were not merely empty words: they reflected a real fact, i.e. society without classes. To put is shortly, our present conditions are much worse than those in which capitalism in the West made its start: there were natural historical prerequisites of its historical development while we are starting actually empty handed.

This process – capitalization of Russia in conditions of declassed society both socially and culturally – was not initiated by Gaidar's government in January, 1992 and even not by the Perestroika of Gorbachev. Without going deep into the history, leaving aside the shadow of Peter the Great who is sometimes called the first Occidentophile, we have all the ground to relate our specific "Westernization" with the reforms of Alexander II.

It is known that these reforms were the response to the urgent necessity but the response was not quite optimal, meeting only part of the necessities. Like in many other major episodes of the national history, the situation was most typical of Russia: state initiative accompanied by poor development of the social movement. The reforms of Alexander II were in fact transformations from the top. They manifested one of the most important consequence: the traditional classes – nobility and peasantry – began to disintegrate as classes, new classes – bourgeoisie and the proletariat – formed slowly and with great difficulty, becoming "classes for themselves" only in half a century. The transition from feudalism to capitalism, initiated by the 1861 reform. What is most curious is that now like then, too, the reform was preceded by a six-to-seven year "epoch of openness". Today, too, the state is the initiator of the reform (to the extent it is capable of). However, the present "human material" immediately identifies the ugly cynic forms, which the "emerging bourgeoisie" often takes.

In this connection one cannot help but recall the behests of the convinced Occidentophile – "unrestrained Vissarion", that is Belinsky who, at the end of his life, unexpectedly came alive from socialist dreams and began to defend the bourgeoisie from the attacks of Herzen and Bakunin. One may also recall other Occidentophiles – from V. Botkin to P. Struve – who sounded almost to the tune, asking God to let us have bourgeoisie.

Despite our personal dreams and strivings, we more and more became Occidentophiles.

We will limit ourselves with these statements of the victory of Occidentophilism in the dispute with Slavophiles over the last century and the half but let us not forget in any way the experience of Occidentophilism in

Russian thought which offered various versions of the "chemical way" (to use the word of D. Pisarev), that is evolution towards capitalism.

There is yet another reason why we should remember that there has been no abstract West of any kind.

It is now the fact that Germany and France, Great Britain, the USA and Sweden as well as Japan and South Korea which are also regarded as the West, like many other developed and not so developed capitalist countries all had their own way and specific features. The fact is that the multifarious experience of the Western countries was tried to fit to Russia as far back as the 1840s by many representatives of Occidentophile thought, although not straightforward. This is a tremendous unconquered ideological area that we are still to digest.

* * * * * *

Creeping into the world of private enterprise, criticizing the old, still called socialist, system, ridding ourselves of the fetish of the "communist perspective" and the slogan of "socialism with human face," let us not ignore the socialist heritage of national Occidentophile thought, scrutinizing the critique of inner maladies of present bourgeois society.

The Western world has transformed since then, advancing far ahead in many respects, especially in the field of material well being. It healed up many former maladies, opening new sources of its being which have never been known before. But it seems there is something left in it which the 19th century Occidentophiles criticized and which is still subject to critique.

What is curious impersonal culture, called "mass culture", is progressing; the intellectual artistic consumerism imposes its will to the artists more and more, which is becoming a problem in our country, too.

The individual freedom remains limited by public opinion, standardizing not only the individual's conduct but also his thoughts and feelings - all this goes in conditions of prosperity and democracy of the most advanced forms of political organization. "The golden mediocrity of the petty bourgeoisie", as Herzen put it.[23]

---

[23] A.I. Herzen, op. cit., Vol. 10, . 209.

What has remained and even consolidated is the reverse side of democracy: the "dictatorship of the majority", the dominance of the majority over a single individual, which is no better than any other dictatorship, ethically and spiritually. Herzen's, like others', critical arrows, aimed at the Western way of life, may still be effective even today.

This exposes the conventional character of the very notion of Occidentophilism, which necessitates singling it out or making prominent because there were Westerners and Occidentophiles. Of course, some advocates of everything that was European were averse to the relativity of those economic and sociopolitical institutions so desired by them. Next to it was making absolute, willingly or not, the bourgeois values. Regarding these conceptions, Chernyshevsky wrote: "If we think to what extent may of the so-called Occidentophiles are aware of what is good and what is bad in Europe, and that many of them still regard as best what is worst in Europe, we will have to admit that the critique of the European life borrowed by Slavophiles, directly or not, from the best modern thinker, is far from being useless to improve our understanding of Europe."[24]

But according to other Occidentophiles, the contemporary bourgeois system is merely most optimum in the particular conditions and for the given moment; a form of society which is alas not an ideal organization of economic, social and political set-up. Humanity is still very far from the perfection.

This is admitted by many Western authors like Zbigniew Brzezinski who said in an interview to *Komzomolskaya pravda* (January 4, 1992) that the world lost its ability to create, think and generate ideas. It became impoverished spiritually: there is a danger that the mankind, having become lazy, may turn into a crowd of well-groomed and well-fed but absolutely futile machines. People must understand that there are things in the world, which are vitally, more important than a microwave oven, a personal plane or smoked sausages.

In the 1770s the education ministry of Prussia was headed by Baron Zedlitz. This "short educated despot"[25] suggested to his subordinates a thought

[24] N.G. Chernyshevsky, *Collected Works*, in 15 vols., Vol. IV, Moscow, 1948, p. 727 (in Russian).
[25] A.V. Gulyga, *Kant*, Moscow, 1977, p. 95 (in Russian).

that they should respect philosophy. He was convinced that after graduation the student should be a doctor, a judge, a lawyer, etc. or, to put it another way, work for several hours a day but be a human being all his life.

It tallies fairly well with the maxim of our best Occidentophiles. What is even more remarkable is that the instruction of this "short despot" answered most explicitly the question "What are we to do?"

What we really are in need of is people, convinced like that Baron of Prussia. With good reason Immanuel Kant dedicated his book *Critique of Pure Reason* to him.

Change of Civilizations and the Historical Fates of Russia[*]

L Abalkin (Academician, Director of the Institute of Economics, RAS): The problems of civilization development, long-term tendencies, patterns of the cyclic movement, crisis factors seem to become one of the major topics of our theoretical studies.

The scientific community feels more and more the necessity to elaborate a new paradigm, a new way of understanding the realities of today's world, its past and future. I would define several questions, which, to my mind, deserve special attention of experts.

First, can one interpret the developments in Russia without any relation with the changes in the evolution of human civilization at the end of the 20th century? Now more and more of the leading scientists of the world community feel worried about acute crises that have swept all human civilization. This particularly relates to the issue of post-industrial society. There are numerous well-grounded estimates that such a model of human civilization can hardly be implemented as a whole and this does not relate only to the group of the leading

---

[*] This article was published in Russian in the journal *Voprosy ekonomiki* No. 8, 1994. It includes exerpts from reports given at an interdisciplinary conference in March 1994.

countries. In any case, one can hardly imagine the development of civilization as a single process.

Second, both the programmes of the discussion and the reports widely used the notions of "civilization" and "civilizations". But nevertheless, the set of categories and concepts has not been elaborated fully. What I mean is either the civilization is a synonym of human society beginning from a certain moment of its historical development when society passed the stage of barbarism and savagery or this notion is a series of historical stages but different than the traditional formations: agrarian, industrial and post-industrial civilizations.

The notion of civilization has also another meaning, which describes not only the temporal aspect but that of space, too. These are the historical types of civilized society. Their classification is fairly well covered in scientific writings. If one implies such an understanding of civilization and tries to find out the place of Russia in global processes as a special type of social structure, one should not forget such names as Nikolai Danilevsky and Lev Gumilev. One cannot either avoid the analysis of the works by Arnold Toynbee and Arthur Schlesinger, Jr.

And lastly the third one, to what extent are society, political forces and movements free in their choice of the model of future development and to what measure is the model programmed. At this point we again get back to the eternal question of the correlation between the genetic and teleological approaches, and the goal setting. On the one hand, the margins of this freedom may be preset by certain regular progress in technological cycles, and, on the other, there are possibly certain types of civilization which are motivated by history, culture, morality, values which may also preset the margins of the choice although they may vary to an extent.

Yuri Yakovets (Academician, Russian Academy of Natural Sciences, vice-president of the International N.D. Kondratyev Foundation): Now it seems we have approached the general regularities of the historical process and their specific manifestations in the past, present and future of Russia. Let us clarify the conceptual tools.

We shall understand a *historical cycle* to be a period of time between one change, a qualitative leap in the history of an ethnos, a state or the whole of humanity and the next crisis and the beginning of the next stage in the endless wave-like spiral movement. The historical process is polycyclic: the historical cycles of various duration and depth overlap each other in the development of each country and in world history. Leaving aside the current fluctuations and the casual ups and downs of history, a range of intermediate cycles, let us single out the four principal types of historical topics:

– the mean-term cycles with an amplitude of oscillation of about ten years, which coincide, with the widely known economic cycles;

– half a century cycles (the Kondratyev cycles) related with the change of generations, technological modes, the principal assets or with the changes in economic, socio-political and cultural relations;

– century-long cycles which manifest themselves in the periodic (once in several centuries) change of world civilizations right through their multilayer structure;

– millennium supercycles which cover several related civilizations.

All these cycles overlap each other to form a general historical rhythm, which accelerates, compressing historical time. Estimates testify that each civilization that follows is 1.5 times shorter than the previous one. But the movement is not regular even within each historical cycle; the course of time accelerates in periods of crises and revolutionary upheavals and slackens during the phases of maturity and stagnation.

Society's genotype becomes richer, following the laws and patterns of social genetics – those of heredity and selection. The nucleus of heredity in each historical cycle remains unchanged, altering at the stage of transition to the next cycle and adapting itself to the qualitative shifts in the environment, which guarantees the survival of humanity in its integrity. A transitional period is marked with growing mutations, a partial restructuring of the heredity nucleus, the disappearance or recession of the elements that have become obsolete, and the appearance and consolidation of new leaders. This provides for the stability of the historical process, making it quite flexible and adaptive.

The epicentres of historical changes are not stationary; now and then a people or a region changes its social status and becomes a leader, compelling others to follow its suit. Former leaders yield to new ones, being pushed to the periphery of world progress.

The rhythmic pace of history is cognizable and predictable, expressing the common laws and tendencies, which can be singled out from the past and foreseen in the future. But the historical time is irreversible. The historical progress is under the impact of contradictory factors and becomes the resultant of the multitude of individual and collective vectors, manifesting the effect of people's will and action – on the surface the historical being is reigned by chance.

The study of the major landmarks in the world history allowed identifying seven civilization cycles which, in turn, can be brought up into three supercycles in accordance with similar principles (genetic nucleus) or a civilization:

– civilizations of the ancient world: Neolithic, early slavery, antique;

– emergence, formation and prosperity of industrial society; early feudal, late feudal (pre-industrial) and industrial civilizations;

– post-industrial civilizations, which will start from the 21st century and will possibly cover the first half of the third millennium.

How can one assess the modern stage of the historical progress? Humanity found itself a difficult but interesting phase of historical development when the trajectory of society's motion changes and when the critical phases of the four types of historical cycles overlap each other. The last turn of this significance was manifest a millennium and a half ago when the Roman Empire collapsed.

Defining the major landmarks of the future civilization, one should take care to avoid attractive pictures of the ideals most desired. Society is slow to respond to changes. What will predominate in the nearest half a century already exists in reality and not in the rudimentary form. One should depart from the real being in his trial to identify the elements that will predominate in the future, rather than from what it should be (the normative forecast).

Given this approach, we can outline the major margins of the post-industrial civilization, which is already emerging:

– the renaissance of humanism, the priority of spiritual values of the free creative individual, renewed science and high culture, continuous education, and the formation of the neosphere;

– the humanized economy, decentralization, diversification and higher flexibility of the science-intensive production, demilitarization, greater attention to man's needs and denationalization of reproduction based on the cooperation of various socio-economic formations;

– a novel structure of social, national and political relations, more profound social stratification, transition from the totalitarian or semi-totalitarian state to a great variety of multifarious but equal state formations which will meet the interests of the individual and society, protecting at the same time society's property;

– establishment of a unipolar world, disintegration of the world empires, a multi-dimensional integration of sovereign states, based on humane principles, involvement of such states in global affairs.

Russia, like any other country, has its unique fate, its own trajectory of the cyclic dynamics in the past and in the future. However, it is equally dangerous to ignore one's own uniqueness or exaggerate it without noticing that Russia is subject to the common rhythm the historical progress. One may righteously speak about a special type of local civilization, which impregnated many features of the Western, and the eastern local civilizations.

Today's Russia is in the state of transition from industrial to post-industrial society, somewhat lagging behind the developed countries which initiated this transition process in the 1970s. Such an assessment allows making a well-grounded analysis of the modern crisis and the prospects of getting out of it. What is most important is not the crisis per se and the collapse of the sociopolitical system and socialist ideals. The changes involve all strata of society: the individual and his needs, abilities, knowledge, skills, and motivations; the obsolete technological base of reproduction, the deformed structure of the economy, the whole system of socio-political, state and legal relations, and the individual's spiritual world. One shall not limit him with one trend of changes; the whole structure of society is subject to renewal on the lines of making it and the individual above all healthier. That is why the crisis is so painful and protracted; besides the right diagnosis has not yet been made and the treatment only aggravates the malady.

The analysis of structural shifts, made by the International N. Kondratyev Foundation and the Academy of Agriculture on orders from the Ministry of Economics of Russia on the basis of a multi-dimensional reproductive cyclic macromodel has yielded quite unexpected results. The reproductive structure of the economy has worsened drastically over the years of the crisis. The share of the consumption sector in the gross product has dropped and that of the intermediate sector has rise. This means that the attempts to socially reorientate the economy gave the opposite results. The share of the household consumption in the gross domestic product of Russia dropped from 47.7 per cent in 1990 to 40.5 per cent in 1993 while the same figure in the USA rose from 66 to 69 per cent. Given good harvests in peaceful time, the living standards of Russian people have never dropped so drastically. If the present tendencies keep on for two to three years, we are likely to have a social explosion and even a civil war, which may tell on the productive forces, destroy part of the population and put backwards the rest. Once a great power, Russia will be put back to the periphery of the world progress for decades and will in fact become a semi-colony with a dictator regime with immense resources of nuclear and chemical weapons and many nuclear power stations. This will be a menace to the whole of mankind, again initiating a "cold war", and will retard the transition to the post-industrial civilization, if not destroy it entirely. This pessimistic scenario is unfortunately quite real with lots of prerequisites.

But another, optimistic, scenario is also possible. Realizing the extreme danger, society will rally new forces, which will revive Russia. Resting on the remaining intellectual, technological, labour and production potential, on wise political forces and using the support of the benevolent outer world, Russia shall halt the production slump and the state disintegration and will again embark upon the road of renaissance. Given this scenario, Russia may attain stabilization in 1995 and the level of production it had before the crisis by the end of the century to be followed by a rapid rise. Some favourable shifts manifested themselves in 1993.

Which of these scenarios (or some of the intermediate ones, which is more likely) will be effected depends on many factors. Social science scholars are among these factors. It is their duty to identify the deep-going processes and tendencies of the development in the world and Russia and submit to society and the political leaders the convincing picture of the possible future course of the modern civilization and the transition to postindustrial civilization.

S. Glazyev (D. Sc., Econ., Chairman of the Committee of the Economic Policy, State Duma): According to the theory of technological formations, worked out by the author in TsEMI, Russian Academy of Sciences, in line with the works by N. Kondratyev and other scientists, each long wave of changes hinges on the life cycle of the relevant complex of technological processes which involve various industries and related production means and represent a reproductive integrity. Over the last 300 years five technological formations became known in the history of the technological evolution of the world economy (for more detail see S. Yu. Glazyev, *A Theory of Long-Term Technical and Economic Development*, Moscow, 1993). Each of the formations is related with two long pulses, which make one wave. The new technological formation only begins to develop, dominated so far by the previous formation. The old technological formation is gradually replaced by the new one in two to three decades when the economy goes into the state of structural depression. The general aggravation of the market situation gives birth to radical innovations, creating conditions for the proliferation of basic technologies of the new technological formation. As a result, the economy stabilizes, initiating the next cycle of the long-wave rise.

In conditions of the modern world economy the life cycle of the technological formation covers about a hundred years and it may be represented in the form of two pulses, the first pulse corresponding to the phase of formation in unfavourable conditions when the previous formation dominates, the second pulse constituting the phase of growth. The latter follows the structural reshaping of the economy, induced by the dominating technological formations and is characterized by the favourable market situation and the high rate of economic growth. This phase lasts about two decades and is accompanied by the emergence of the new type of social consumption. The growth of production stimulates reduction in production costs, which involves a change in the price correlation and the growing demand. This multiplier evolves over the whole technological chain in the phase of growth up to the saturation of the relevant type of social consumption and until there is no opportunity to improve the technologies of the new technological formation. The effect of the growth multiplier does not cease immediately, which results in excessive accumulation of resources ending in the impulsive reduction of production over the whole technological chain. When the technological formation reaches the upper limit of growth and the profit begins to drop, a massive redistribution of resources is started in the technological chain of the new formation. As a rule, the substitution of technological formations requires certain social and institutional innovations that sublate the social strain or constructively canalize it, laying ground for a new technological formation and the corresponding type of consumption and the way of life.

A major result of the recent studies was that it proved the technological multi-structure of the Soviet economy. Contrary to the countries with the market economy, the institutions in our country, which regulated the reproduction processes in the system of the centralized management of the economy, did not provide for the substitution of technological formations. The system of centralized planning did not possess the in-built mechanisms, which ousted the obsolete technologies, although the system coped well with the proliferation of new technologies. As a result, the economic decisions made at top level were altered now and then to change the priority of the technical and economic development of the country. This was manifest in the corresponding plans, the institutional changes and the amendments to the structure of capital investment• • • • • • • • • followed the usual old trend of economic development. The economic revival consisted in restoring what had been destroyed. In this way the technological multi-structure was reproduced for the second time and in the 1950s the part played by the third technological formation grew significantly in the economic structure of the country. The fourth technological formation was also significant to a large extent. The country adopted a programme for the proficient utilization of chemistry, oil extraction and refinery grew rapidly. In addition, we initiated a campaign for computerization and extended production of electrotechnical products. Beginning from the 1960s the fifth technological formation began to take shape. By the end of the 1980s we had a distinct, technologically multi-structured economy, each technological formation being reproduced independently.

The production of one technological formation was not closely related with another formation. The departmental system of management of the economy provided certain autonomy of reproduction in what regards large complexes of related production which did not depend on each other, which led to disproportions in the economic structure – a rise in the share of raw materials branches and the drop in the quality of products. The economy suffered great losses at junction points of the technological formations. The quantities of obsolete hardware were piling up. The newly produced values do not allow sustaining mere reproduction. The country did not have enough means to maintain economic growth and replace old technologies.

What happened as a result of liberating the economic life in 1992? The economic relations, which sustained the distribution of resources according to the technological formations, were broken and their reproduction ceased. The whole system was based on the military-industrial complex, which incorporated mainly the fourth and the fifth technological formations. Price liberation and the disintegration of the system of centralized management disorganized the basic relations in the reproduction system. This resulted in drastic changes in the flows of resources redistribution. Among the most vulnerable were the production facilities of the fourth and partly the fifth technological formations which were orientated mainly to the state demand and were not related practically with export, except for the export of raw materials and some types of weapons. The necessity of their products was not determined by the population's solvent demand, being wholly dependent on the state purchases. When the price liberation was coupled with the macroeconomic stabilization as the main trend of the economic reform, which implied drastic reduction in the state expenditures, the production of modern technologies of the fifth formation met with sales difficulties.

Today it is impossible to provide the economic growth on the basis of the traditional type of production of the fourth formation, let alone the third one.

Therefore, as for the priorities of the long-term development the liberation of economic activity should be accompanied by active state support of the branches of the fifth technological formation because the shock was too great for the MIC to stand. At present, practically all technologically formations entered the phase of disintegration, which manifests itself in the degradation of the indicators which show their development at macrolevel as well as in the general indicators of the production efficiency. From the point of view of the technological structure our economy passed to the stage of chaotic destruction. On the surface we have inflation and the slump in production but there inside stoppages of enterprises, a decline in production capacity and practically no innovation and investment activity.

In most cases this is the result of the privatization programme that has been adopted. It destroyed the elements of economic activity, which recently supported the reproduction of progressive technological structures. The main result of the current economic policy is the destruction of technological structures and the gradual closure of the production facilities in all industries. The time has come when the fate of an enterprise is determined by an opportunity to enter the world market and find access to the international finances. But the majority of the enterprises have no chance in succeeding in this. Being tied up with the rigid cooperation with major technological structures within the country which develop independently, the enterprises are unable to adapt to the requirements of the world market without financial assistance in the course of one to two years. It seems to me that from the point of view of the technological evolution we are moving towards the economy's deindustrialization and converting it into a raw materials periphery of the world economy.

So far, it is still possible to curb the crisis but the possibilities are not as many as they were in 1992 and 1993. We can save the most prospective enterprises of the fifth technological formation (the aerospace complex, aviation, and science-intensive technologies in instrument building). The gas industry is the only sector that is well off. It is clear that, given the current inactivity of the state in curbing the crisis, the economy may be utterly incapacitated in the long run, losing all chances of further growth. This will inevitably result in the population's degradation, disintegration of the education system and other spheres, which determine the long-term economic development. But the main political forces are well aware of the dangers of the economic collapse. Given the impotent state institution which cannot attain social agreement and control the executive power, we will not be able to gain any success because any attempts of the active state interference in economic processes end in failure, meeting with corruption and irresponsibility of the personnel for the decision-making in the system of executive power.

M. Titarenko (D. Sc., Philos., Director of the Institute of the Far East, RAS): The disintegration of the USSR and the crisis of relations of more than 35 entities of the Russian Federation led to the extreme aggravation of ethnic relations in the former USSR territories and Russia, too. Involving more than 100 aboriginal peoples, Russia is experiencing a complex and tragic period in its history.

The tsarist policy of invasion, Stalin's despotic terror, the negligence of specific ethnic features and traditions, and inattention to the problems of interethnic relations led to the accumulation of interethnic strain which was aggravated by the Russification of other people's culture. However, the tsarist and the Soviet power took into account the positive role of the Russian language and Russian culture – one way or another they introduced the backward national periphery to the world civilization, mutually enriching at the same time the cultures.

At present, the interethnic conflicts became aggravated in many regions: the Baltic republics, Moldova, Georgia, Azerbaijan, Armenia, Tajikistan, in the Western region of the Ukraine, in the Crimea and some other regions. The former communist dictatorship was replaced with the nationalistic dictatorship, which is even more intolerant of other people's beliefs, infringing the rights and freedoms of national minorities. The ideas of the priority of the aboriginal nation became absolute. Society reiterated the 300-year long discussion between the Westerners and the Slavophiles. Now it is the result of the national crisis, finding the ways of Russia's revival, the necessity to improve the federal relations between the nations and consolidate the equitable cooperation, national originality and sovereignty.

Such discussions are current in Japan and China. A similar situation is typical of the countries which lag behind the world progress but possess enough will to live and try to overcome the national crisis and make fast advance. In their search for the way of modernization and their own strategy of progress these countries critically compare their national experience and the experience of other peoples.

It is exactly the period that Russia is now living through. We are now facing the necessity of finding our own pattern of the renaissance, which would sublate the extremes of Slavophilism and Westernism. It seems to me there is a paradigm of this kind. The first attempt to overcome the contradiction between the Western and the originally Russian, Slavonic and Eastern elements in our Russian civilization and the mentality of Russians was made in the 1920s-1930s when a number of renown Russian thinkers in exile put forward a concept of Eurasian features. We find among them such figures as Trubetskoy, Karsavin, Savitsky, Vernadsky, Gumilev and others.

Naturally, nobody insists on the mechanical repetition of these concepts. What I mean is filling this term with new contents because we have no other term, which could embody the synthesis of two civilizations. What we mean is new Eurasian features. But some old ideas should be preserved. Trubetskoy emphasized that the cultures of all peoples were equal. Each minor culture is unique and its contribution to the civilization is also unique and indispensable. There are no great and minor races, peoples and cultures. The world civilization exists as a "constellation of cultures" of various peoples, regarded Karsavin who considered the interaction of civilizations a "symphony of civilization".

If we follow the way of unifying cultures, suggested by some Russian and Western political and culture scientists, we will tread directly to the war of civilization of which professor Huttington spoke. Such views in the United States and in Western science are sharply criticized. American economist and political scientists Dahrendorf directly calls such views of culture unification a variety of "cultural imperialism". Many scientists hold that the continuing imposition of American mass culture retards the development of national cultures and the progress of humanity, and provokes conflicts between civilizations and ethnoses.

The concept of the Eurasian theorists predicated on the principles of humanism, democracy, equality of peoples and human rights. They regard the world civilization as polyphonic and multicolour. And they are right in the main thing because we do not have so far an integral entity of general human civilization. We can speak about it as an aggregate of national forms of civilization – Russian-Slavonic, American, Chinese, Arabic, Islamic, European, Japanese and so on.

The current Eurasian tendencies do not mean that Russia is departing from Europe but, rather, that it recognizes a balance of European, Western and Asian trends in Russia's policy. The neo-Eurasian tendencies assert the general human values and allow overcoming the Messianic features of the old Eurasian concept and Slavophilism.

The Eurasian paradigm makes it possible to harmonize interethnic relations and regard the cooperation with the Western and Eastern neighbors as a source of and stimulus to mutual development and beneficial cooperation. It seems to me therefore that the Eurasian concept as an all-national Russian idea in no way means a departure from the West or a sort of opposition to it. On the contrary, it promotes openness to both the West and the East.

The experiences of other nations prove that this approach is right. What is one of the reasons for the successful Chinese reform? It consists in the policy of openness, which helped to overcome the age-long seclusion. Another reason for China's success resides in combining the programme of transformations with the idea of reviving China's national dignity.

We will be able to cope with our current problems only if we manage to formulate the common national idea, which shall be organically combined with the idea of Russia's revival and reformation. Once Stolypin said that the seed of reform would be fruitful if it was sown in the national soil. And it seems to me that the new Eurasian concept is this national soil.

A TENDENCY TO ECONOMIC REINTEGRATION IN THE CIS

Vadim Kirichenko[*]

W hen I wrote this article I first though to name it "A Change in the Landmarks in the CIS" to emphasize an evident turn in the relationship between the former Union republics from the economic separatism in the first years of the Commonwealth to intentional efforts to intensify integration in the economic domain. However, the objective assessment of the actual disintegration that has taken place, the discrepancies of the particular interests that manifested themselves, and the real difficulties that arose in the new conditions of economic relations between the countries preclude outright conclusions. Experience testifies that we have to go a long way, usually a hard one, from the goals, solemnly proclaimed, and the real positive results. Therefore, I chose the academic form of the title, which implies a weighted analysis of the new phenomena and the difficulties, and contradictions that may arise in the course of their implementation.

* * * * * *

[*] V. Kirichenko, D. Sc. (Econ.), Professor, Deputy Chairman of the Russian Federation Committee for Economic Cooperation with the CIS Member-States. Specializes in the theory of reproduction and methodology of economic forecasting. This article was published in the journal Svobodnaya mysl, 1994, No. 9, in Russian.

After the USSR had fallen part, the economic relations between the former republics underwent radical changes: market relations replaced the economy within the single economic complex, which was coordinated mainly by directive methods of planning. This process of marketing exchange is characterized by unusual dynamism, which is often spontaneous, and is accompanied with economic losses for all the participants. Their intentions and practical deeds may unpredictably alter within the shortest periods of time.

The outcome of the single ruble zone may be an example of this. The logical course of developments of disintegration in the monetary-credit sphere going on in 1992-1993 was unexpectedly interrupted in September, 1993, by signing six agreements between the states on the creation of the ruble zone of the new type. But the real life and the differing economic interests bring about opposite result: by the beginning of 1994 the CIS has developed many national currencies with intermediate monetary means. April 1994 brings a new turn: Russia and Byelorussia come to an agreement to unify their monetary means on the basis of the Russian ruble. Further developments showed that the agreement remained a slip of paper.

Such an instability of economic policies of the states and the evident difficulties of transforming one type of relations into another prove that the process is extremely contradictory. To my mind, this instability predicates on one phenomenon, which embodies both the results of the development during the previous decades and the challenges of the post-Soviet existence. On the one hand, this is the effect of the economic and technological dependence of the economies of the newly formed states which so far cannot develop independently of each other, and on the other, the formation of the proper national interests of the state and the inevitable divergence of interests, required by the political sovereignty. Hence the more complex, and somewhat contradictory, political and economic situation which makes it difficult to bring about a positive result. Whatever the ups and downs were in the former USSR territory, a tendency prevailed to continue economic divergence, followed by the state and national. The fundamentals of the former Union integration, however contradictory, were falling apart one after another although they were quite acceptable in the former system of relations between the republics within a single state with a single economy but utterly impossible in the new emerging system of economic relations between the states.

The economic divergence and disintegration manifested themselves primarily in that the state broke the traditional economic ties and curtailed the mutual exchange. Thus, the goods turnover between Russia and other CIS members amounted in 1993 to about a half of the 1991 goods turnover. In 1992 compared with 1990 the share of Russia's neighbours in the foreign trade exchange dropped 1.8 times in exports and 1.3 times in imports. The structure of exports has drastically become worse: the share of output of the oil gas industry as well as the ferrous metallurgy grew substantially while the share of machines, equipment, means of transport and light industry products dropped. The disrupted economic ties were one of the factors that caused a recession and economic crisis in the CIS (including Russia).

Besides, this broke the single ruble zone and the common price system owing to a differing price liberation to be followed by the disruption of the common market of goods and services owing to various tariff and non-tariff limitations of foreign trade, and the loss to the homogeneous system of economic management as a result of the differing progress of market reforms. What was most essential was the differing principles of the macroeconomic policies conducted by the states, primarily in the financial and monetary and credit spheres, and the particular trends of the structural policy. Thus, practically everything that characterized the economic space of the USSR as a single whole has been eroded in the shortest time.

The creation of the CIS allowed to somewhat coordinate the relations of its participants by bringing it into the framework of a regular legal process of agreements, and attain some positive effects on the multilateral basis in the political, humanitarian and defense areas. But multilateral agreements brought about poor results in the economy: the real life was based on bilateral agreements. Unfortunately, one comes to the conclusion that the CIS as an economic integration grouping has not worked yet.

This is natural. At first, the former republics were busy dividing the Union heritage and "nationalizing" its lumps, protecting its inner market from the neighbors and searching independently for an access to the world market. The integration had to wait.

However, it soon became evident that the newly emerged states could use the former Union wealth (finishing production lines in machine building, chemistry and petrochemistry, the military-industrial complex, lines producing sophisticated consumer goods, objects of the transport and electric energy infrastructure) only if they co-operate with other members of the former whole. Uncoordinated passes at the world market only aggravated the terms of trade for all the members of the CIS.

The processes of economic divergence have not been completed yet and it seems they will continue although not in such an uncontrolled manner as before. One may suppose that they have passed the peak of confrontation. Therefore, the CIS is turning more resolutely to the ideas of integration and consolidation of economic ties, at least at the level of intentions.

This point of view was propped by the false conception that if the countries freed themselves from the "voracious" centre this would automatically bring a rise in the material, financial and currency resources in each country that formed in the ruins of the USSR. Besides, each member of the CIS began to better understand that it fell into a profound socioeconomic crisis, that isolated measures of stabilization would bring no positive effect, especially bearing in mind the fact that the hopes for lucrative assistance from the advanced countries and easy access to the world market separately had no ground. The change of moods was facilitated, among other things, by the factor of the acute political situation within the newly formed states, including the dissatisfaction of the majority of the population by the isolationist policy their leaders were conducting, the negative consequences in the socioeconomic sphere which were brought about by the voluntarist action in toppling down the USSR as a "geopolitical reality" that was actually unprepared legally and economically.

All CIS countries now realize that it is impossible to climb out of the crisis and solve the urgent national economic problems independently. By trial and error, the countries found out that the maintenance of economic ties is the prime prerequisite of stabilizing the economy.

However, the hopes of the opponents of economic isolation who believed that the former economic ties would automatically be kept up also failed. They hoped that these ties are so strong and stable that they were capable of puling by inertia the chain of economic integration even in the conditions of political sovereignty of the former Union republics. It so happened that there are alternatives and automatism does not always work. Experience testifies that it is possible to retain and rationalize the current economic ties only as a result of purposive coordinated actions of the countries, taking into account the modern political and economic conditions.

The positive effect of the resulting developments was that all countries realized that the economic relations in new conditions can be built only taking into taking into account the mutual interests on the market basis rather than pursuing one's own interests on the unilateral basis, following the principle of political and national bias, to put it another way, following the criterion of economic effectiveness and interest.

This fully refers to Russia, too. However, Russia's situation has certain specific aspects.

At the moment of the USSR's collapse and during the initial time of the CIS creation the Russian leadership was strongly influenced by an idea which was not advertised but was advocated by the new Russian establishment: to make a fast advance and leave others behind. The Russian leadership did not believe that the majority of the former republics were ready to start essential political and economic transformations. Russia allegedly had to reduce to the minimum its commitments to the former Union republics, to free itself from the burden of the Big Brother of the conservative still pro-communist regimes in order to gain the freedom of maneuver for the outstanding democratic and economic reforms. It should not care much about retaining the former ties because other countries were most interested in them than Russia and they would have to follow suit. Foreign official and non-official advisers gave similar recommendations.

However, Russia failed to make a fast advance. It seems that the proponents of this concept failed to take into account a lot of essential circumstances that made this concept unrealistic. What matters most are geopolitical losses Russia made as a result of the disturbed balance between the political and military forces in the world. By the end of its existence the USSR lost its traditional props such as the world communist and workers' movement, the national liberation movement of the former colonies, the socialist camp and especially the CMEA countries turning their face to the West. As a partial compensation for these losses the authors of this concept counted on the support of the national democratic movements in the former Union republics. But unfortunately, many representatives of these movements turned to be the staunch carriers of anti-Russian moods, striving for isolation. When the USSR fell, Russia faced a real danger to be separated from the world in the Western, Southern and SouthEastern directions.

Many of the new states announce themselves a "bridge" for Russia to Europe and Asia but each of them may turn to be a check-point with strict rules. The situation may appear more realistic if one reckons the experiences Russia had when it tried to transport its cargo to the West via sea ports beyond its territory or using oil and gas pipelines.

The political instability and military hostilities in a number of new states, easy penetration through the outer borders of the former USSR do not allow Russia to remain care-free and leave the zones of higher risk for it may aggravate the security problems. To avoid the undesirable course of developments the situation may require additional material, financial and human resources.

One should not forget more than 25 million Russians who appeared overnight beyond the bounds of their country. Russia could not be indifferent to their economic, social, civil and political fate. The best legal means of support of the Russians who found themselves abroad is to resolve all the problems with the former Union republics on the beneficial basis for many years ahead.

Lastly, the economic realities. Russia began to build new economic relations with the former Union republics after essential losses in its economic, scientific and technical potential. As it appeared the economic reform did not yield so far any positive result to improve the economic might of the country. On the contrary, the country's might continues to deteriorate in the course of the crisis. The social price of the reform turned to be extremely high and its social base narrowed.

Thus, according to a number of factors the theory of "fast advance" as a boon for Russia turned to be groundless and harmful from the point of view of our long-term interests. It seems we cannot regard that we have overcome it. Equally, we cannot accept the political rhetoric of the great power stand, which is voiced even at the level of power structure of Russia. Extremes are dangerous. Real politics should proceed from the necessity for Russia to make a large-scale effort to organize various beneficial relations with the new states as equal partners. Life poses a strategic task of providing and maintaining a benevolent, politically stable and economically beneficial environment around the whole of Russia. In the economic domain we will have to coordinate our current measures with the tasks of the long-term strategic perspective which leads to economic consolidation and a new integrated community of sovereign states. The socioeconomic and political climate in the Commonwealth as a whole and in separate states has changed under the impact of failures instigated by isolation tendencies, the lasting crisis and enormous social losses, induced by the economic reforms. The countries turned from economic isolation to consolidation.

* * * * * *

The new period in the CIS development can conventionally be started from September 1993, when the treaty of economic union was signed in Moscow. The treaty put forth a perspective goal of restoring a single economic space with the free exchange of goods, services, capital and labour. The treaty was signed by all countries of the Commonwealth (including the Ukraine as an associate member).

In fact, it was the first large-scale instrument of the CIS, which put forth a concept of building a new system of economic relations between the countries that signed the treaty. It lays ground for a coordinated long-term strategy, pivoting on the economic integration.

Whether this period is successful or not depends on how the countries observe the ideas and approaches disclosed in the treaty.

First of all, it is a complex instrument, covering all significant areas of the economic domain of the countries: trade, monetary, credit, financial and currency relations and the production cooperation.

Secondly, the treaty envisages that such complex mechanism as the real large-scale Economic Union shall be formed in stages. Each stage should undergo an all-round preparation with due account of the mutual interests and the real situation. No stage shall be by-passed.

Thirdly, it is envisaged that the countries shall move from the simple to the complex, from the elementary forms of integration to more advanced (e.g. from a multi-currency system to a currency union, from relations, based on free trade via a customs union to the common market).

Fourthly, the concept agreed upon in the treaty shall be implemented as a series of particular agreements on minor issues, which will form later the real image of the Economic Union.

Fifthly, emphasis is laid on future coordination and even unification of domestic economic policies of the member-countries of the treaty, and on convergence of the economic legislation.

Giving a positive assessment to the treaty, I shall add that it is motivated mostly by urgent tasks to normalize the trade and economic relations between the CIS countries. However, the Economic Union is short of more fundamental and perspective ideas, which, according to the world experience, should make the basis of a long-term integration grouping. What I mean is the ways of optimizing economic relations between the countries by way of the structural reshaping of the economies of the member-countries, the issues of interacting with other integrated groupings, finding and protecting their stand in the world economic ties. Lastly, the cardinal problem, which determines the viability and prospects for an integrated grouping in the modern world, consists in solving the tasks related with passing to the new stage of the scientific and technical progress and in promoting the required technological breakthroughs. All this shall yet be elaborated.

However, let us get back to the present matters. The signing of the treaty made the activity of the CIS institution, and primarily its supreme bodies – the Council of Heads of State and the Council of Heads of Government – more goal-oriented. Their meetings in Ashkhabad (December 1993) and Moscow (April 1994) had on their agenda issues of signing a set of agreements, which, one by one, will set the framework of the Economic Union. In particular, each such agreement should be filled up with joint practical actions of the CIS states.

The treaty of economic union is not of course a dogma but a mere designation of the principal of lines of development. It is possible and even necessary to make amendments with the changing situation, depending on the real progress in the actual integration. Such amendments may be made in the form of particular agreements. Even given good intentions, the negotiations on particular problems may not be simple.

An example of this is the progress made with regard to the approaches to creating a permanent body of the Economic Union. Originally, such an organization, named the "Economic Committee of the States" was meant to be effective in the Councils of Heads of State and Government and have certain supranational functions. As a result of the April 1994 Moscow negotiations it was turned into a commission of the Economic Union under the Coordinating Consultative Committee (at vice-premier level) and its function to make mandatory economic decisions were put to doubt.

I should underline that we talk about the creation of an economic union rather than the real union. The treaty is only a starting point in the long way to a full-scale union. There is no reason for wishful thinking, regarding a good document as a reality.

* * * * * *

One should bear in mind that the proclamation of intentions to attain the economic consolidation of the CIS and even the signing of the treaty of economic union do not remove the outstanding contradictions and difficulties in the Commonwealth. The assessments of the contradictions vary from state to state, which tells on their stand, changing now and then, and which undoubtedly will manifest it in the course of multi- and bilateral negotiations.

From Russia's point of view, the main contradiction of the current economic cooperation with CIS countries is inadequate economic relations and the imbalance of trade with the majority of the countries as well as the lack of export and import prices parity. Russia's balance of trade with the republics was positive even at times of the USSR. But at that time it was a domestic problem of a single state, which was solved mainly by administrative methods by redistributing the financial resources. Now the problem has changed both qualitatively and quantitatively: it turned into a problem between the states which is solved on the market basis, assuming a larger scale.

In 1993 the trade balance of Russia was positive with the majority of the CIS countries (except Azerbaijan and Uzbekistan), the export surplus amounting to more than 5 trillion rubles (38 per cent of the Russian export to the CIS). More than 70 percent of this imbalance amounted to the Ukraine, 18 per cent to Kazakstan, 4.5 percent to Byelorussia, which was equal to 50, 41 and 11 per cent respectively of their import from Russia. The situation is aggravated by deferred payments for the products supplied.

In order to maintain the required volume of goods exchange Russia gave credits to the CIS countries in 1992 and 1993. When the technical credits of the Central Bank of Russia were converted into the state credits it was agreed in the bilateral negotiations to write the resultant debt. As of October 1, 1993 the sum amounted to 2.2 trillion rubles or, according to the agreed exchange rate, 4.8 million dollars. In 1994 the practice of crediting was continued, although in smaller volumes. The uneven trade and payment balances had a negative impact on the intensity of trade between the countries. At the same time this motivates a rigid stand of Russia in defending its economic interests.

The economic ties within the CIS framework are under strong pressure from the changing price rates. By the moment the CIS was created the level of prices for the goods of the Russian traditional export with respect to the world prices was lower than that of prices of goods imported.

According to the IBRD data, in 1991 the level of prices for oil with respect to the world prices was 13 per cent, 9 per cent for gasoline and diesel oil, 3 per cent for natural gas, 31 per cent for nickel, 5 for fertilizers, 6 for cement (Russian exports), 63 for cotton, 71 for wool, 49 for vegetable oil, 83 for zinc and hardware thereof, 45 per cent for copper and hardware thereof (goods received by Russia from the former Union republics).

Naturally, such a deformed system of prices in the relations of countries that are now independent is not always followed. The countries are now moving towards the world prices. As the starting conditions differed, and Russia regulated its prices for energy carriers for a long time, this brought about the effect of price dotation to the close neighbors of Russia or, to put it another way, the effect of conventional losses for Russia (conventional in that sense that the price was compared with the world price). According to the estimates of the International Monetary Fund, this latent price dotation amounted to 12,000 million dollars in 1992. In 1993 the situation changed as the prices approached the world level.

According to the data of the Centre of Economic Demand under the Russian Federation Government, the prices for Russian exports to the CIS grew 12 times for oil, 15 times for gas, 6 to 7 times for gasoline, diesel oil and fuel oil, and 6 to 7 times for trucks and cars as compared with the level of 1992. As a result, the correlation between the mean prices for exports to the CIS and the contract prices for exports to foreign countries also changed as calculated in rubles according to the mean rate. Over January-September, 1993 the correlation amounted to 43 per cent for oil from the level of contract prices and 38 per cent for gas.

Although there are objective reasons for these phenomena in trade and payment relations, one can easily see the negative impact on the intensity of trade between Russia and other members of the CIS. They are unfavourable for the integration intentions. In particular, the existing differences between the domestic and world prices for fuel and energy result in that Russia has to maintain the export tariffs on them. The overall rates of price rise, especially the prices for fuel and energy resources, exceeded the possibilities of the production enterprises and foreign trade bodies to adapt to the new price situation.

In such a situation Russia's multi- and bilateral relations with the CIS countries are motivated by Russia's stand in defending its own economic interests. Given the strict conditions at macrolevel, Russia may improve the balance of payments with its partners but the general volume and intensity of economic ties is likely to be affected. In such conditions Russia should not cross the margin which may bring about losses at microlevel (suspension of payments to the enterprises for the products supplied to the CIS countries, reduction in the production output because of shortages in supplies of raw materials and component parts, shortages of food supplies, loss of markets for some goods).

These contradictions may be settled if the non-tariff limitations in the foreign trade are lifted, if the tariff limitations are reduced or lifted on the mutual basis, if favourable zones are created (like in the case of the agreement of production cooperation). Other ways of removing contradictions consist in finding alternative means of paying trade and economic debts (turning them into lease payments for using various facilities, into transportation payments for cargo transit), in appropriating property (directly or through shares). In all cases mutual compromise is required, including on the part of Russia, too, which will allow to realize the possibility of stabilizing the economy by retaining the economic ties, restoring the opportunities of rationizing relations between the countries. Naturally, the compromises we mean should go to that extent which would make the desired stabilization possible.

Consideration of the particular contradictions allows tackling the general problem: one should admit that the CIS countries are not united in their assessments of the favourability of the Economic Union, especially the immediate effects of its implementation.

The nearest task for Russia is overcoming the problem of correlating the economic relations with its partners from the CIS, restoring the required economic ties, forming production and commercial structures between the states as new forms of organizing economic relations and integration at microlevel. To my mind, this can be done already on the basis of bilateral agreements, which can take into account specific features of each country.

Russia regards the Economic Union as a prospective form intensifying cooperation with partners (also as a means of multilateral integration) in the institutional, structural, investment, scientific, technical and foreign trade policies (with respect to the third countries and other integration groupings). In the strategic aspect Russia is interested in converging the CIS into a full-fledged international organization of economic integration.

At the same time the majority of the CIS countries are interested in intensifying multilateral relations to joins efforts in attaining the nearest goals (mostly thanks to easy access to Russia's fuel and energy resources, easy-term crediting of the trade turnover and debt payments, retarding the process of transferring to the world prices, lifting the export taxes and non-tariff regulation of Russia's fuel and energy resources). One may be sure that their interest to the treaty of economic union is based on hopes that using this union they will normalize their, trade and economic relations, restore the broken ties and overcome the crisis, stabilize the economy, and make the transition to market easier.

The stand of many CIS countries in terms of strategy is doubtful. In future they will be more interested in becoming less dependent on the production and the market of Russia and other CIS partners, in finding alternative sources of financial and material sources, technological donors of their markets. One can neither exclude the possibility that the integration intention may become looser.

Such a discrepancy between the current and future interests, the tactical and strategic goals, stemming from different levels of economic development, will undoubtedly complicate the general movement to the Economic Union. But it is better if this problem is taken care at once and as a whole than it is solved in its unexpected manifestations in particular cases of the treaty process.

It is also important that the process of trimming the economic relations after the USSR disintegration is taking place in new conditions. What is essential in that case is that the former republics are sovereign politically and possess the status of independent states which are solving their political and socioeconomic problems to meet their national and state interests; the transition to the market relations and methods of regulating their domestic and foreign economic ties is irreversible; the administrative functions of the state have

Vadim Kirichenko

markedly diminished in the economic domain and the enterprises have become the independent economic entities, solving their economic problems in their own way, including those with other countries. Besides, the process of disintegration has gone rather far, which has been mentioned above.

Therefore, when realizing the treaty of economic union the countries will have to reorganize the economic mechanism of integration. Formerly, it was formed vertically: the top bodies imposed a certain system of relations through the Centre. Under new conditions the horizontal ties between the production and commercial units become of prime importance, because the real and stable integration may be implemented only at microlevel in the course of cooperation between real economic entities: enterprises, joint stock companies, banks, investments bodies, etc.

The economic mechanism of integration imparts greater importance to the elements, which have the international character. In case of the multilateral cooperation the greater part may be played by the transnational production and commercial structures – joint ventures and stock companies of any kind. The advantage of structures of this kind consists in that they integrate economic bodies of various countries according to the principle of economic expediency and are largely independent of political fluctuations or ambitions and the relations between the states.

The structural basis of integration also requires remaking. Not a single republic of the former USSR was satisfied with the obtaining structure of the economy and the degree and direction of the development of its economy. The economies' defects were mostly manifest when the single Union complex fell apart. It appeared that the economic structure of the majority of the republics did not fully correspond to the requirements of economic security, the needs of the population and the honourable introduction into the world market, and did not meet the new national goals. What is objectively urgent is respecialization of the economy, changes in the commodity and geographic structure of the foreign relations and ties, and overcoming the orientation towards solely the CIS economic space without any alternative. All countries of the CIS are interested in controlling this process within the framework of an economic union.

To attain success in the structural reshaping one condition should be met by all means. First of all, Russia will have to elaborate a concept of the relevant transformation of its economy. It should define zones in which it should create, restore or expand the capability which would allow it substitute for the import from its nearest neighbors, and adopt measures to consolidate the production cooperation in the regions in which it is not reasonable economically to set up national import-substituting capacities. Lastly, what will be necessary is to identify areas in which there is no alternative to imported products. This could be a good basis for cooperation with other CIS members.

We may assume that, as a result of the structural reshaping and stopping the irrational trade exchange the volume of exchange will diminish. But more effective ties will undoubtedly compensate this and it is this factor, rather than raising gross volumes, will become more attractive to the partner countries.

* * * * * *

To sum up, I would add that nowadays there are no simple ways of economic unification. One cannot merely repeat the past experience. An image of glass vessel comes to my mind at this point. If it fell broken, and there is a natural desire to restore it, there are two ways. One can collect the broken pieces and glue them. It will have the same form, although with visible traces. There is another way. One can remelt the glass pieces and then cast a new vessel, having the same or better form, but in any case intact and strong. The second way is more progressive.

The realization of such an approach implies first of all maintaining the existing ties between the former Union republics on the usual scale as an important measure of stabilization of their economies (reintegration in the narrow sense of the word). At the same time we should ensure in the near future the rising qualitative transformation of the economic cooperation between the new states, meeting the mutual balance of interests and the economic benefits of such a consolidation on the basis of market methods and the principles of economic relations between the countries, accepted now in the world (reintegration in the broad sense of the word as an evolution of integration ties in new forms).

This also defines the urgent measures of realizing the treaty of economic union of the CIS countries. The new states should come to an agreement to lift the tariff and non-tariff limitations in accordance with the agreements in effect about the zone of free trade and further develop the conditions of trade in line with the principles of the customs union. This in turn implies that the countries should create a unified system of regulating foreign economic ties and essentially converges the mechanisms of regulating the economy as a whole and harmonize the foreign trade policy with respect to the third countries. In the sphere of payments and settlements the states should without any hesitation work out the mechanism converting their national currencies on both the bilateral and multilateral basis and initiate the operation of the Interstate Bank for settlements between the states. In the field of production cooperation the states shall have in due time to prepare programmes of joint investment, specialization and improvement of the production structure, form the financial-industrial groups promoting the complex technological systems, create transnational economic structures with employment of all forms of property, effecting integration at microlevel.

In that case the integrational commonwealth of the new states will enhance the effectiveness of the economic complexes of the countries and the integration grouping as a whole, and correspond to both the national and the collective interests of the Economic Union.

INDEX